The Ocean

Nature's Cycles

Earth's Layers

PLANET EARTH

for Curious Kids

An illustrated introduction to the wonders of our world, its weather, and its wildest places!

The Environment

Natural Disasters

ARCTURUS
This edition published in 2022 by Arcturus Publishing Limited
26/27 Bickels Yard, 151–153 Bermondsey Street,
London SE1 3HA

Copyright © Arcturus Holdings Limited

All rights reserved. No part of this publication may be reproduced, stored in a retrieval system, or transmitted, in any form or by any means, electronic, mechanical, photocopying, recording, or otherwise, without prior written permission in accordance with the provisions of the Copyright Act 1956 (as amended). Any person or persons who do any unauthorized act in relation to this publication may be liable to criminal prosecution and civil claims for damages.

Author: Anna Claybourne
Illustrator: Alex Foster
Consultant: Anne Rooney
Designer: Dani Leigh
Editor: Becca Clunes

ISBN: 978-1-3988-2020-3
CH010029US
Supplier 29, Date 0722, Print run 00001000

Printed in Singapore

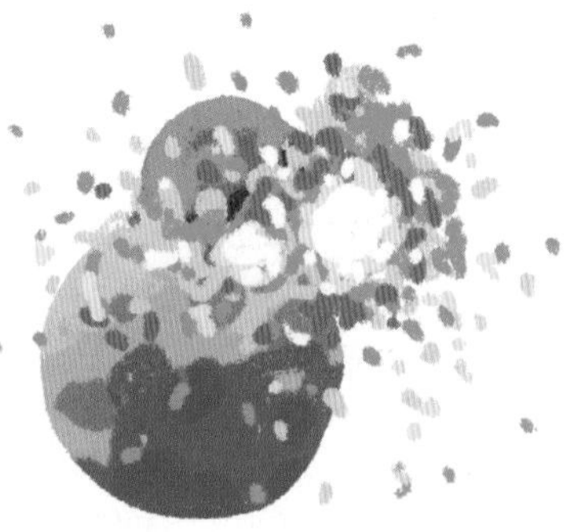

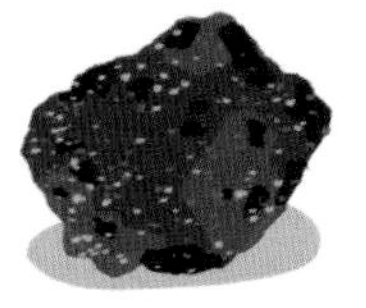

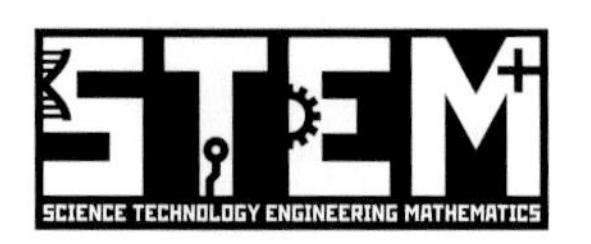

What is STEM?

STEM is a world-wide initiative that aims to cultivate an interest in Science, Technology, Engineering, and Mathematics, in an effort to promote these disciplines to as wide a variety of students as possible.

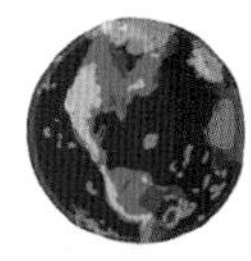

CONTENTS

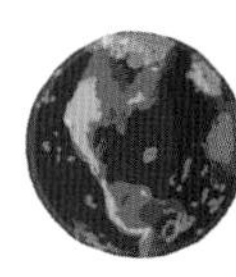

WELCOME TO PLANET EARTH!

Planet Earth is our home, the only one we know. Learning about our world tells us how it began and how it works, how to stay safe from its dangers, and how to make use of its vast resources. From rocks, rivers, metals, and fertile soils to wild forests, mountains, and beaches, our world is full of beautiful places and useful things.

The study of the Earth is called Earth science, and it has many different branches. Geographers study the Earth's surface and how humans use it. Geologists study rocks, minerals, and how the Earth formed. Meteorologists study weather, oceanographers study the sea, and ecologists look at how our planet provides a home for countless living creatures.

Step into the pages of this book to explore everything about our amazing world: its ancient beginnings, awesome minerals, exploding volcanoes, whirling windstorms, landforms, and life forms—and how one species, we humans, have changed it forever.

FLYING THROUGH SPACE

Our planet, the Earth, is a ball of rock flying through space at a mind-boggling speed of 107,208 km (66,616 mi) per hour. That's almost 30 km (19 mi) every single second. It whirls around the Sun, a huge, fiery star 150 million km (93 million mi) away. A year on Earth is the time it takes to complete one orbit.

BIG OR SMALL?

The Earth is both big and small! It seems huge to us, and compared to a human being, it IS huge. It measures 12,742 km (7,917 mi) across, and its circumference—the distance all the way around—is 40,075 km (24,900 mi). If there was no sea in the way, and you could walk around the world without stopping to sleep or rest, it would take you almost a year.

However, compared to the vastness of space, the Earth is TINY. Over a million Earths could fit inside the Sun. Our Solar System, including the Sun, the Earth, and the other planets, is more than 12 billion (12,000,000,000) km (7 billion mi) across.

But the Solar System is just a tiny part of our galaxy, or star cluster, the Milky Way. It contains billions of other stars besides the Sun.

And beyond the Milky Way, far, far away across the Universe, there are countless other galaxies.

ONE OF A KIND

Space is full of stars, and there are many other solar systems and planets. But ours is the only one we know of, so far, that has living things on it. However, some other planets do have rock formations, volcanoes, and weather like we do.

OUT OF CURIOSITY

IT'S A MYSTERY!

Why does the Universe exist, and where did it come from? We study space, planets, rocks, and minerals to help us find out—and we're still working on it. But why things exist at all, no one really knows.

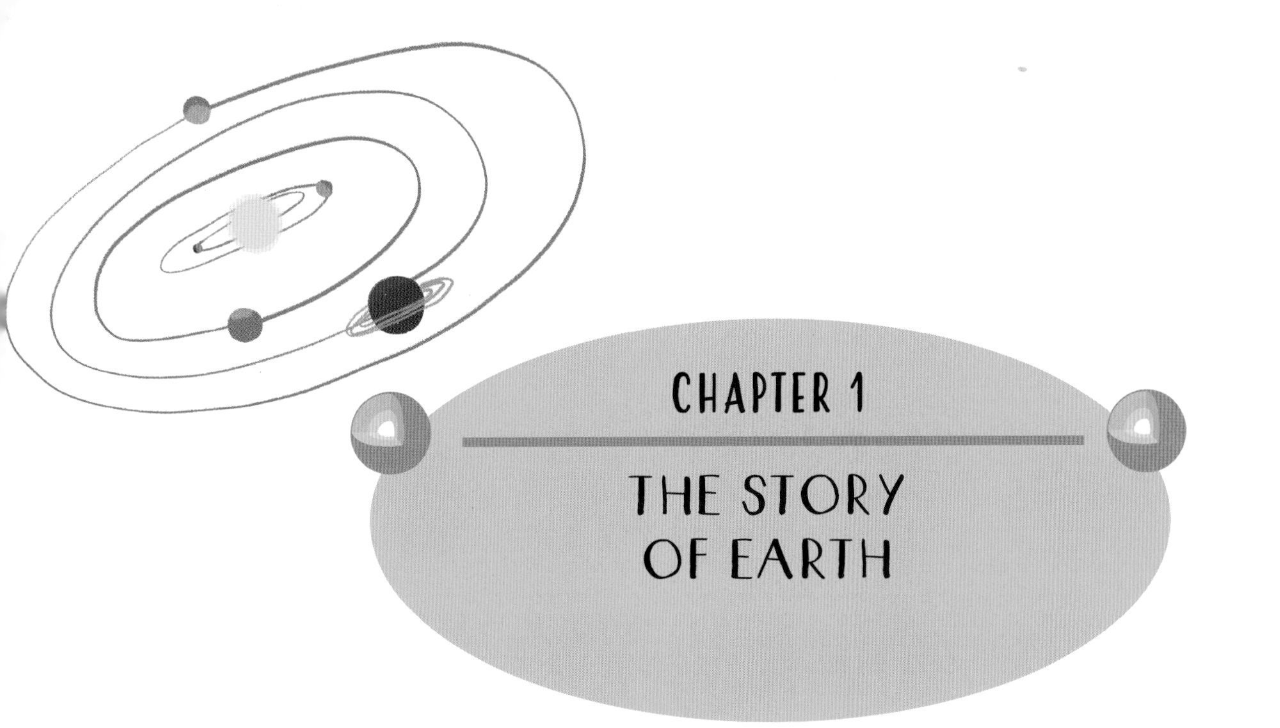

CHAPTER 1

THE STORY OF EARTH

The Earth is very, very old, but it wasn't always here. As far as we can tell, it formed about 4.54 billion (4,540,000,000) years ago from hot dust and gases whirling around the early Sun. Since then, the planet has cooled and changed. It has gained a Moon, a hard rocky crust, and enough water to cover most of it in seas and oceans.

In this chapter, we'll turn back time to see how the Earth, the Sun, and the Universe itself began. We'll find out what the world is made of and how it ended up the way it is today.

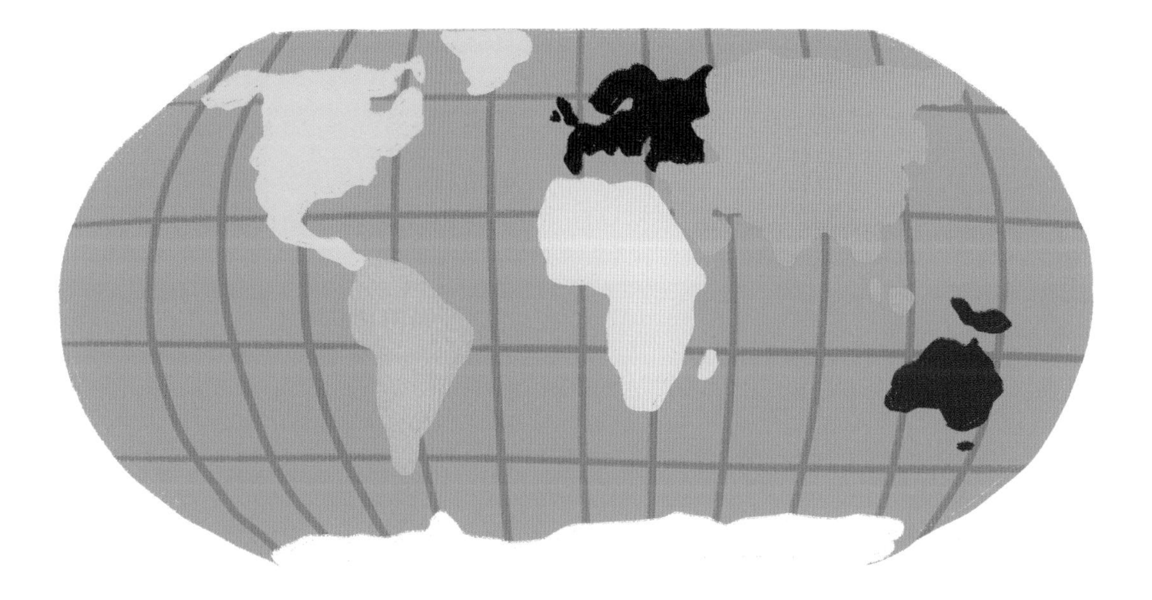

IN THE BEGINNING

Long, long ago—so long ago, it's almost impossible to imagine—the Universe began.

WHAT HAPPENED?

We don't know exactly how the Universe started and the stars and planets formed, since no one was there to see it. We just have the most likely explanations, based on things we can measure and find out now. This is what scientists think happened ...

13.8 billion years ago

THE BIG BANG

At the start of the Universe, all the matter (or stuff) that makes up the stars and planets was concentrated into a single tiny point. Suddenly, it expanded in a huge burst of energy known as the Big Bang.

4.6 billion years ago

THE SUN

Like other stars, the Sun formed from a cloud of gas and dust pulled together by gravity. A flattened circle of hot dust and gas whirled around it.

4.6 billion years ago

THE SOLAR SYSTEM

Gradually, clouds of dust and gas clumped together to form planets.

4.5 billion years ago.

THE MOON

Early in its existence, another planet, Theia, crashed into the Earth. This blasted a large mass of rock into orbit around the Earth, which became our Moon.

OUT OF CURIOSITY

The Moon has fascinated humans since ancient times. In 1610, Italian scientist Galileo took a closer look at the Moon with an early telescope and realized that it had mountains and craters.

And in 1969, astronauts set foot on the Moon for the first time.

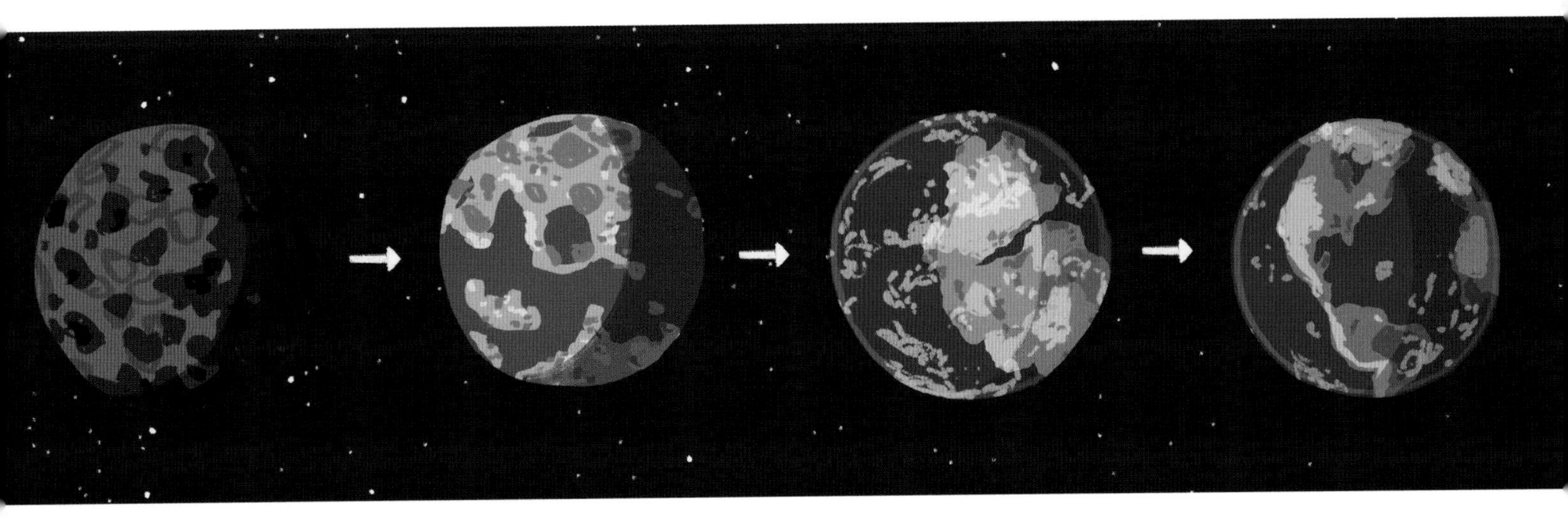

4.45 billion years ago

LAVA EARTH

After the impact that created the Moon, the Earth was mostly hot, molten rock, like a ball of lava ...

4.4 billion years ago

LAND AND SEA

.... but gradually it cooled and its outer layer, or crust, hardened into solid rock. Water collected on the Earth to form the early ocean.

Around 3.8 billion years ago

LIFE BEGINS

The first simple, single-celled life forms developed and gradually evolved into many other kinds of life, such as plants and animals.

50 million years ago

THE CONTINENTS

The Earth's land has moved around a lot over time. By about 50 million years ago, the continents we have today had taken shape.

SEASONS, DAYS, AND TIDES

The Earth orbits around the Sun, and the Moon orbits around the Earth, and the Earth itself spins around and around. These movements create rhythms in our lives, giving us days, seasons, and tides.

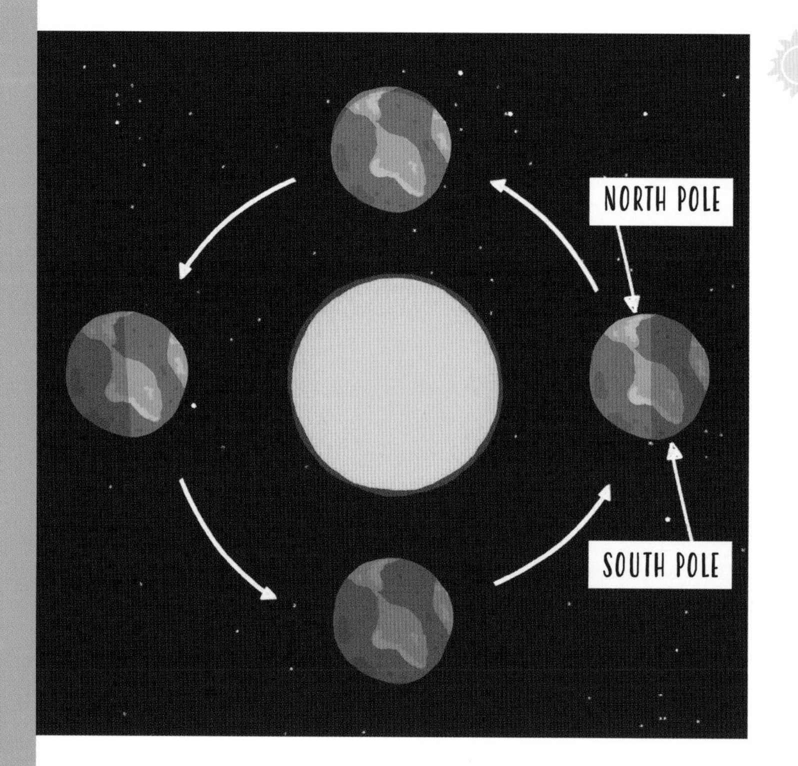

A YEAR OF SEASONS

A year is the time it takes for the Earth to make one full **orbit** around the Sun. As it does so, we go through seasons, which are different depending on where in the world you are. This happens because the Earth is slightly tilted in its orbit.

When the North Pole is tilting away from the Sun, the Earth's northern half, or hemisphere, gets less sunlight. This makes it darker and colder, and it goes through winter.

At the same time, the South Pole is tilting toward the Sun and goes through summer.

DAY AND NIGHT

Meanwhile, the Earth spins around. When your part of the world faces the Sun, you have daytime. When it turn aways from the Sun, night falls. It looks to us as if the Sun rises, moves across the sky, then sinks—but it's really just the Earth turning.

The Earth spins just over 365 times during its orbit, so we get 365 days in a year.

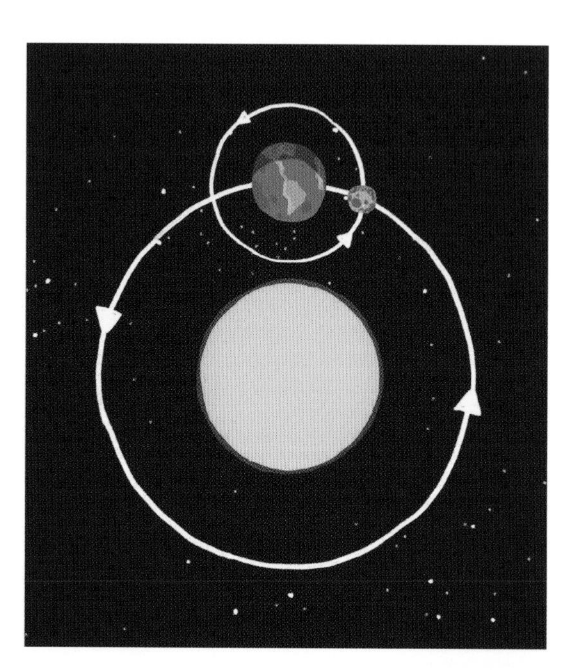

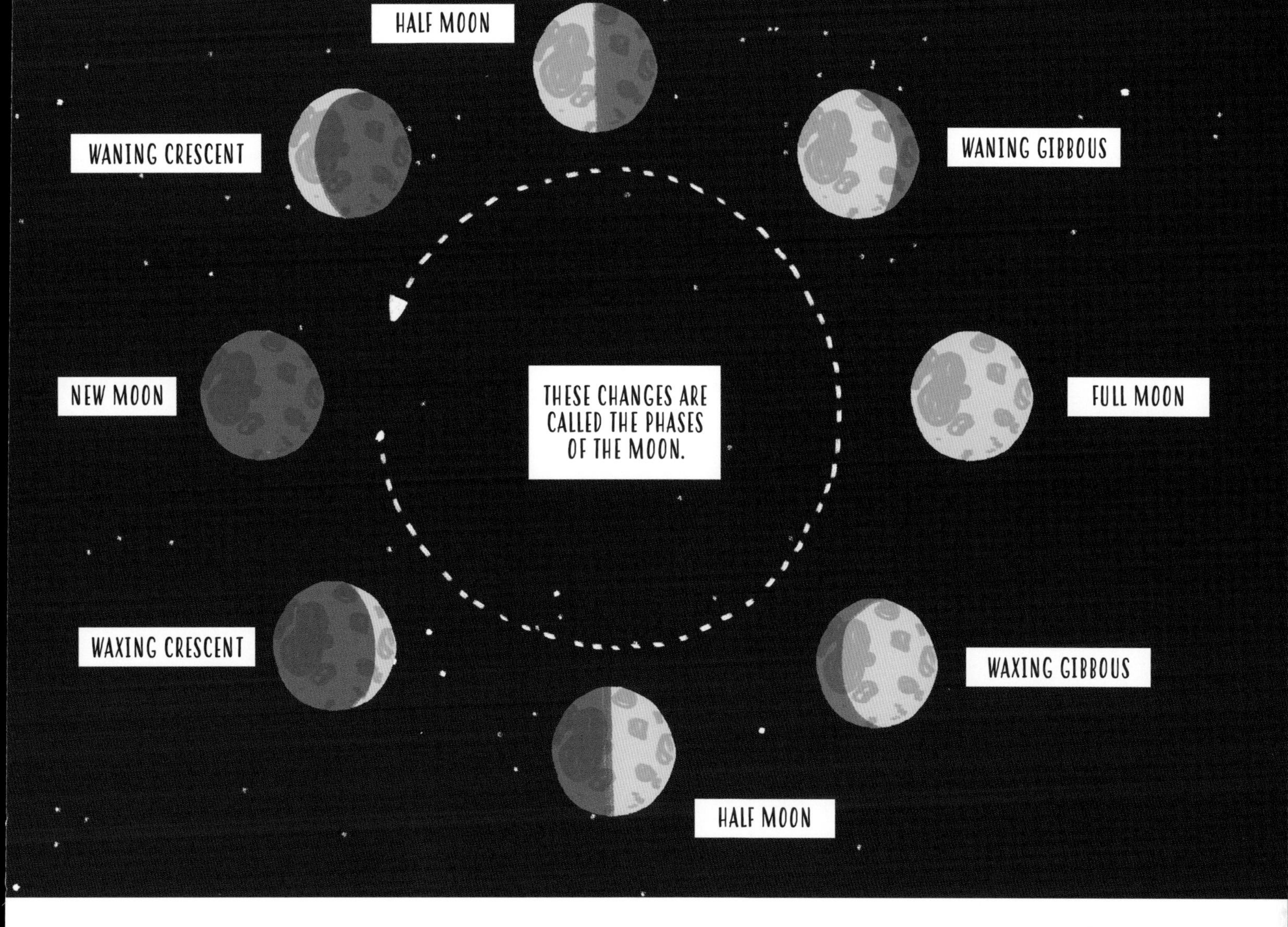

 MOON PHASES

The Moon orbits the Earth roughly once every 28 days. As it moves around, the Sun lights up one side of it, just as it does with the Earth. Through its orbit, the Moon appears to change shape, as we see more or less of its lit-up side.

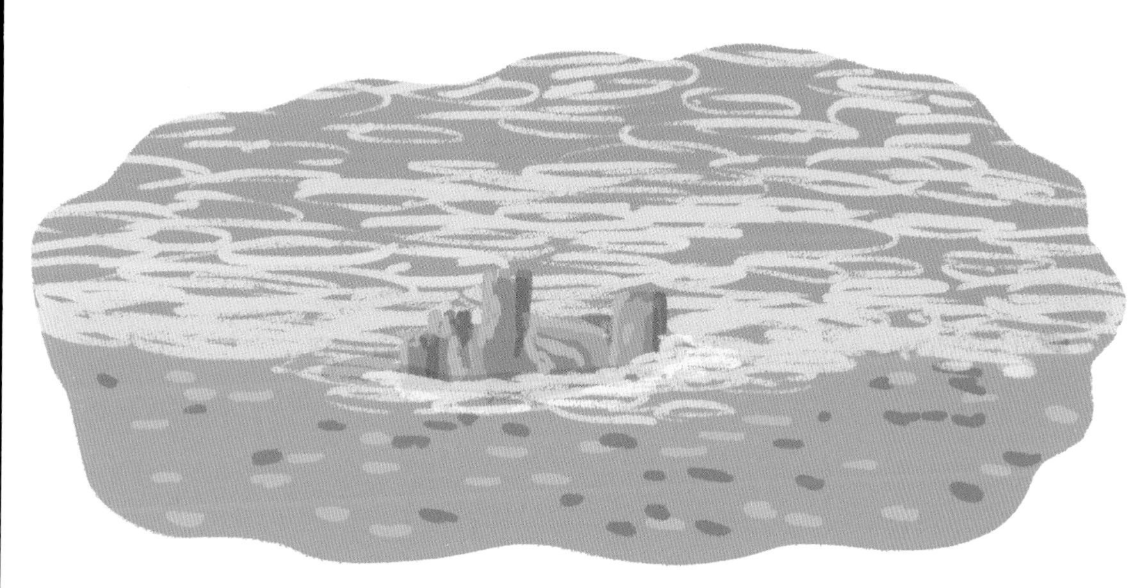

As the Moon passes overhead, its **gravity** pulls on the Earth's oceans. This makes the water move up and down, creating the tides.

LAYERS OF THE EARTH

We live on the Earth's crust, its outer surface layer. Inside, it has many more layers. It's much too hot inside the Earth for us to explore there—but if you could, this is what you'd find.

Ground level to 35 km (22 mi) down: THE ROCKY CRUST

The Earth's **crust** is mainly made of rocks and minerals. It ranges from about 5 km (3 mi) thick under the oceans, to 50 km (31 mi) thick or more where there are high mountain ranges on land.

35 km to 2,900 km (22 mi to 1,800 mi) down: THE MELTING MANTLE

The **mantle**, meaning "cloak," is a deep layer of very hot, partly melted rock. It moves around very slowly like hot, sticky toffee. The temperature of the mantle ranges from around 1000 °C to 3700 °C (1832 °F to 6692 °F).

Near the crust, the mantle is mostly solid, but in some places, melted rock, or **magma**, bursts through the crust and becomes **lava**, forming a volcano.

The deeper, lower mantle is even hotter. But it is also under much more pressure, making it more solid and slower-moving.

2,900 km to 6,371 km (1,800 mi to 3,960 mi) down: THE IRON CORE

The Earth's core, or middle, is made of two metals: mostly iron, with a smaller amount of nickel. Like the mantle, it has two layers. The outer core is more liquid, and it flows and swirls around. This movement is thought to give the Earth its magnetic field.

The inner core is a huge ball of solid metal. It's VERY hot: about 5,200°C (9,392°F).

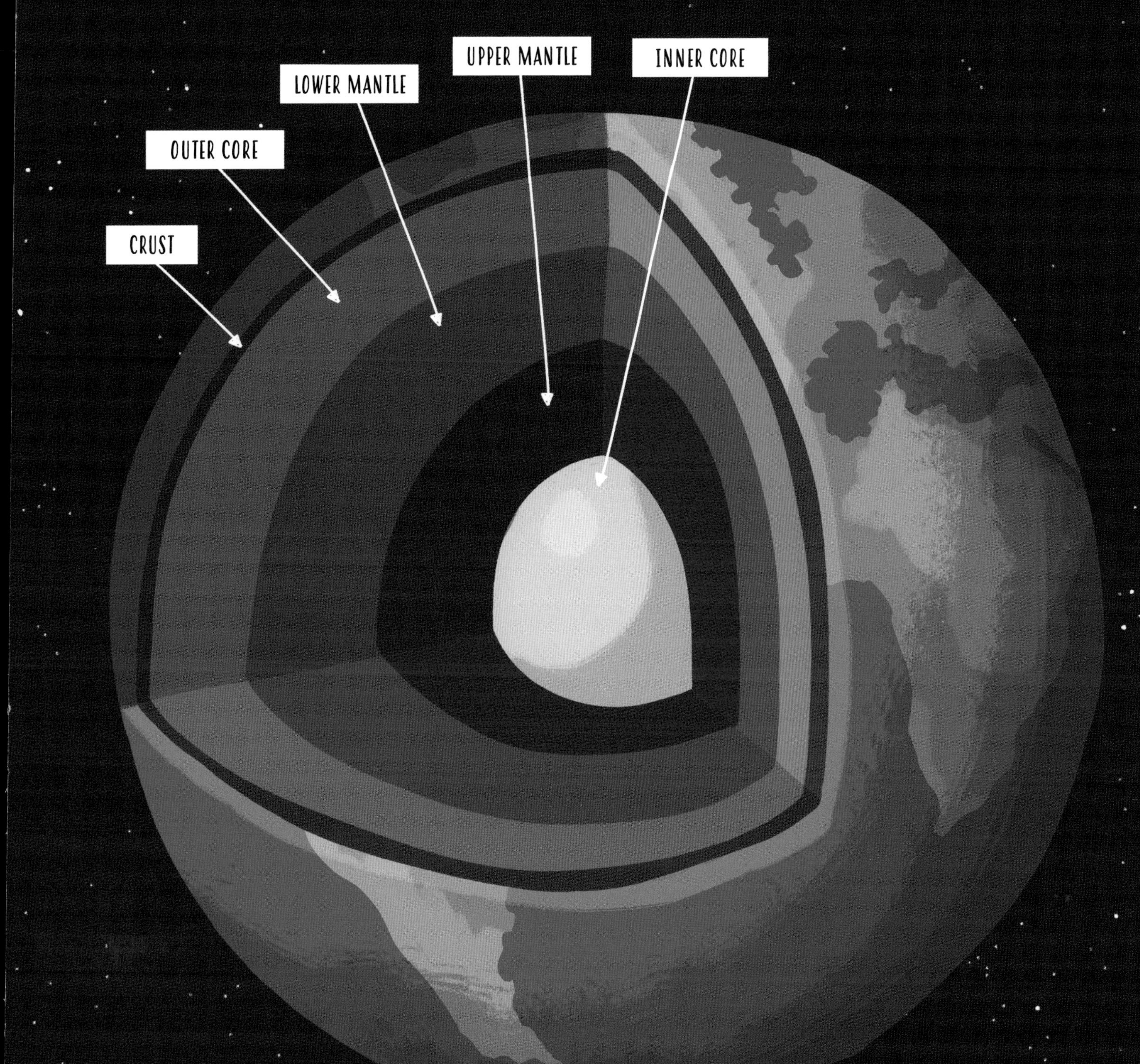

OUT OF CURIOSITY

Why is the Earth so hot inside?

The heat inside the Earth is left over from when it formed from the hot gas and dust around the Sun, billions of years ago. Though the outer crust has cooled, the inside still hasn't. It's like a big baked potato that's still hot in the middle!

CONTINENTS AND PLATES

If you look at a map of the world, you'll see that it has several main areas of land, or land masses. They are called the continents.

THE SEVEN CONTINENTS

We divide the Earth's land into seven continents. Each continent includes the main land mass and the smaller islands around or near it. They are:

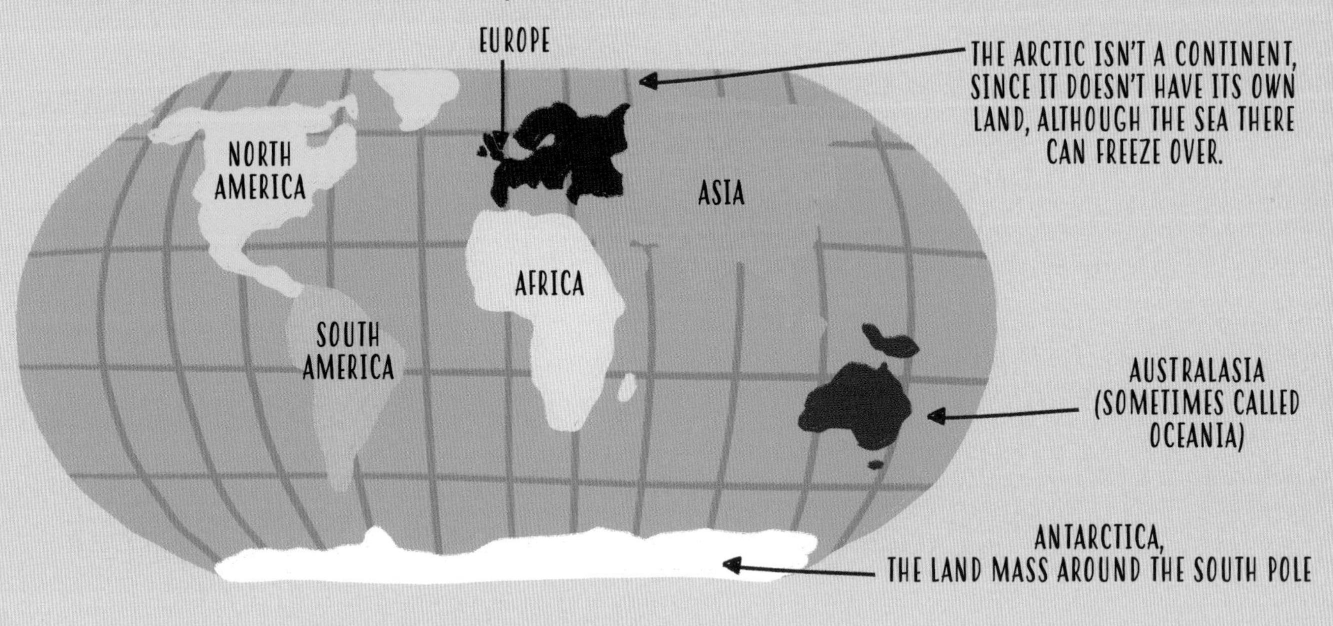

LAND AND SEA

The Earth has continents and oceans because it has two different types of crust in its hard, rocky outer layer.

Continental crust is usually around 30–50 km (19–51 mi) thick and floats on the magma inside the Earth. It's mostly made of granite rock.

Oceanic crust is thinner and denser (heavier for its volume) than continental crust and is mostly made of basalt rock. It lies lower than continental crust, and that's why most of the world's water flows down and fills these areas, forming the seas and oceans.

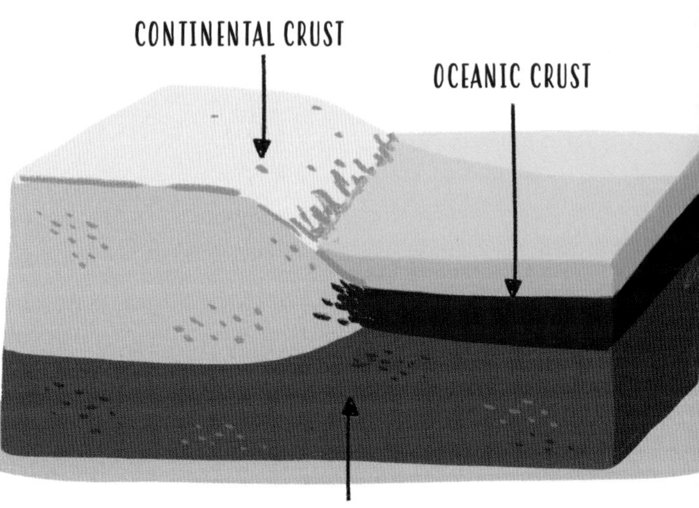

GREAT PLATES!

In the 1970s, scientists discovered that the crust is made up of huge sections, or **tectonic plates**. They fit together all over the globe, a little bit like huge jigsaw pieces.

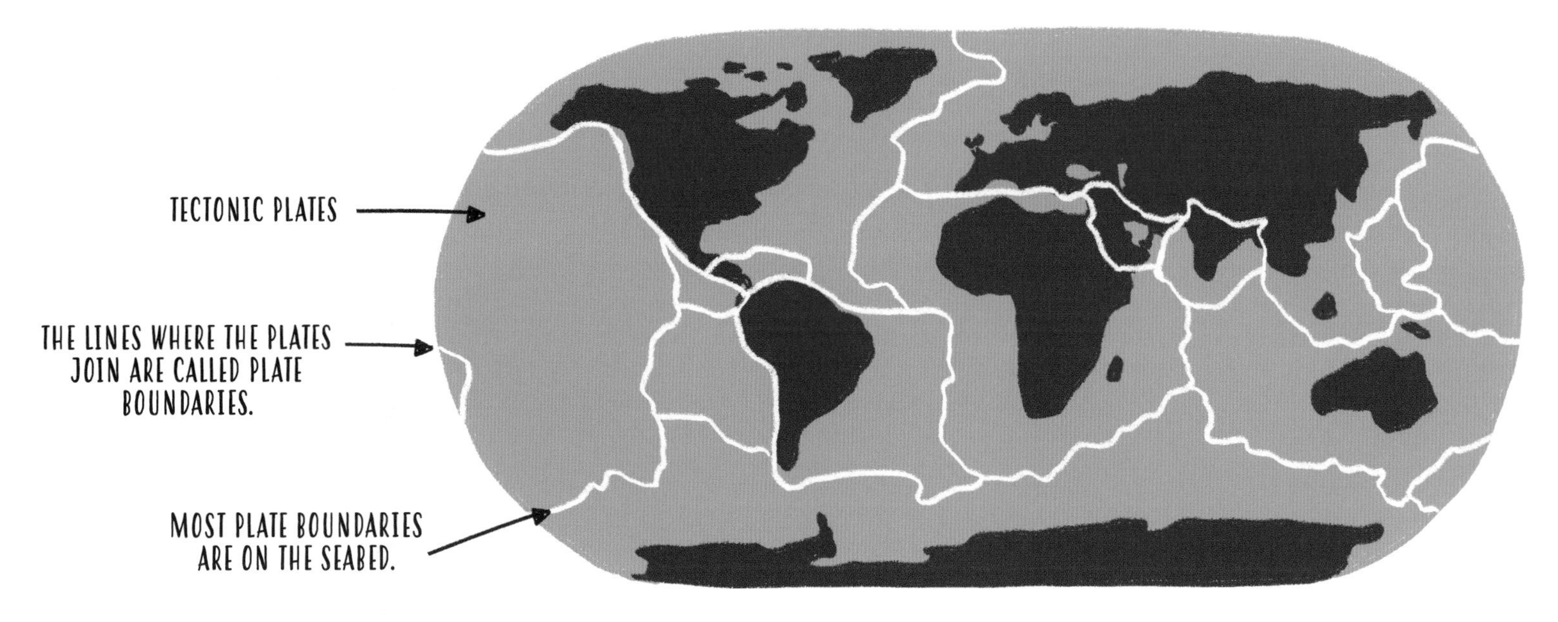

PLATE RECYCLING

At some **plate boundaries**, called **divergent boundaries**, the plates slowly move apart, and magma from inside the Earth moves up to form new crust.

At others, called **convergent boundaries**, the plates push together. Usually, one plate moves slowly underneath another and melts back into magma.

This means that the plates, and the continents on them, are always moving around. But they move very slowly—at about the same speed that your fingernails grow!

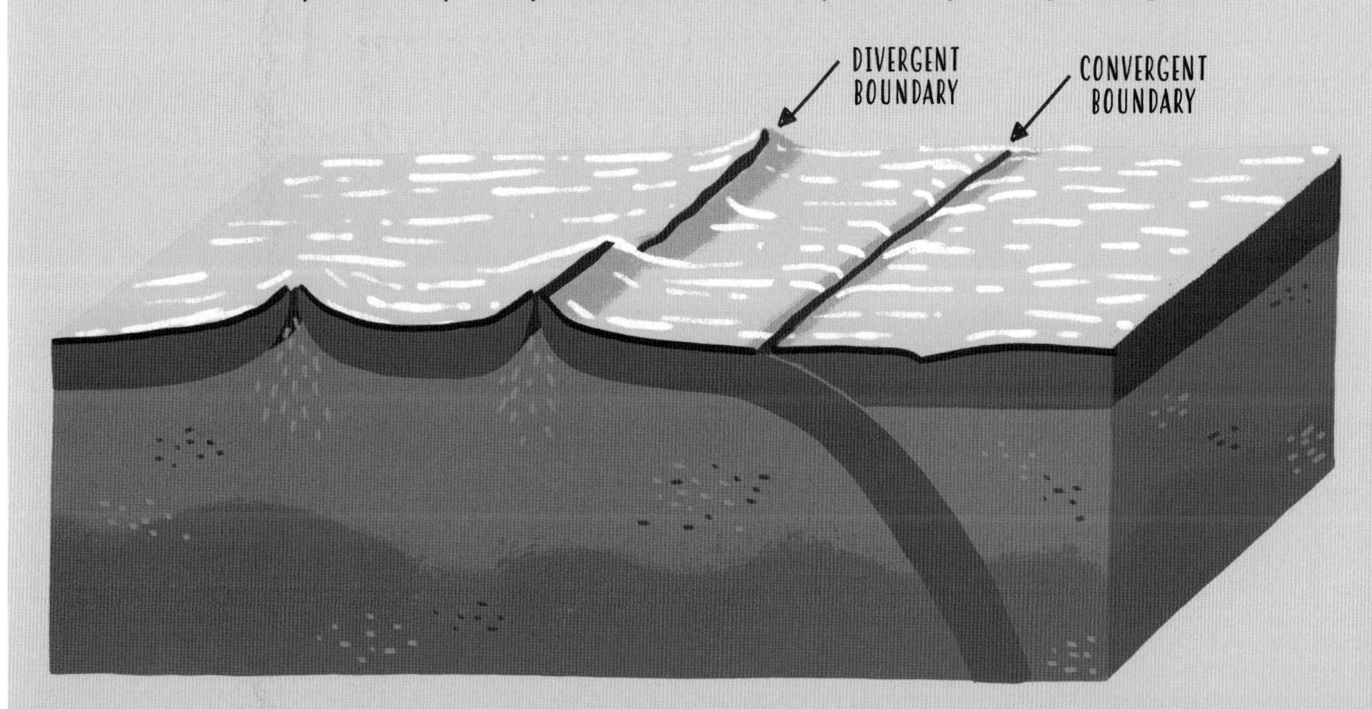

ROCKS AND MINERALS

Rocks and minerals are what most of the Earth is made of. They come in thousands of different varieties, shapes, and shades. And besides giving us the ground we walk on, we use them in countless ways.

WHAT ARE MINERALS?

Minerals are natural, nonliving substances from the Earth that are pure or "homogenous," meaning that they are the same all the way through.

Minerals include metals, such as zinc, used to make batteries, paints, and brass instruments, and gold, used to make rings. Many minerals form gemlike crystals, such as rose quartz (below).

ROSE QUARTZ

WHAT ARE ROCKS?

A rock is made up of a mixture of different minerals. For example, sandstone, shale, and granite rock all contain the mineral quartz mixed with other minerals.

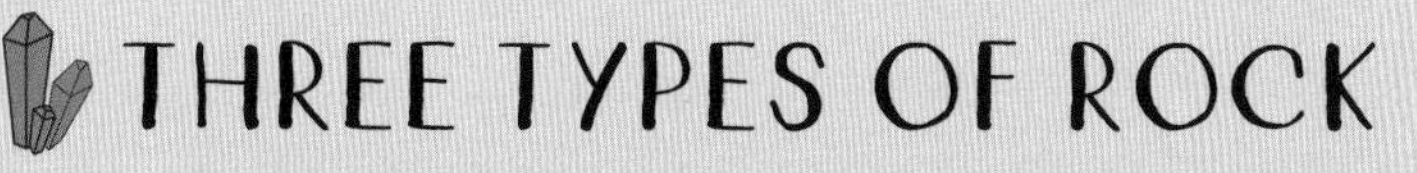

THREE TYPES OF ROCK

Geologists (Earth scientists) divide rocks into three main types, depending on how they formed:

Sedimentary rock forms when layers of mud, sand, or seashells slowly settle and pile up, usually at the bottom of lakes and seas.

SANDSTONE IS A COMMON SEDIMENTARY ROCK MADE FROM LAYERS OF SAND. IT'S USED FOR BUILDING.

YOU CAN OFTEN SEE THE STRIPED LAYERS IN SANDSTONE.

Layers of sedimentary rock form on the seabed. Over time, the lower layers get pressed down by the weight of the layers on top and harden into solid rock.

Igneous rock (meaning "fiery rock") is made when magma flows out from inside the Earth as hot, molten lava. As it cools, it hardens into new rock. Pumice is a type of igneous rock. It has holes in it, caused by gas bubbles that got trapped in the lava as it cooled. We use it to make foot scrubbers!

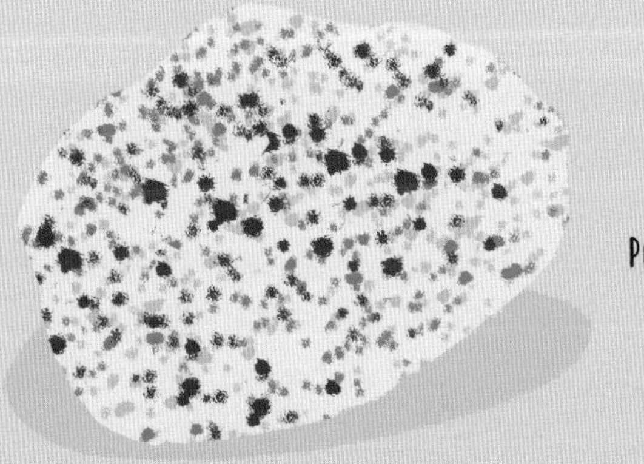

PUMICE

Metamorphic rock (meaning "changed rock") forms when other types of rock get squeezed or heated. This could happen deep in the Earth's crust as the tectonic plates move around, or under a volcano where molten magma heats rocks up.

Slate is a metamorphic rock formed when softer clay or shale rock gets squeezed. It naturally forms flat sheets, which make good roof tiles.

SLATE

THE ROCK CYCLE

Rocks might seem as if they never move or change, but they do. They are constantly being cracked, crushed, dissolved, worn away, or melted, and new rocks form on the seabed or when volcanoes erupt. They move around in a process known as the rock cycle. It's something like the water cycle, but much, much slower.

1 **Weathering** wears rock away and breaks it down into smaller pieces. Rain and rivers slowly dissolve some types of rock. In freezing weather, rocks break and crumble when water in cracks freezes and expands, making the cracks bigger.

2 As rocks tumble and roll around in rivers or on beaches, they wear down and become rounded pebbles.

3 Small bits of rock become sand and mud. The process of **erosion** carries rocks, sand, and mud away through gravity, wind, or rivers. Lots of sand, mud, and pebbles get carried downhill into seas and lakes.

4 Sand and mud settle at the bottom of seas and lakes, becoming **sediment**.

5 Sediment gets squashed down, hardening into sedimentary rock.

6 Where tectonic plates push together, some rock gets pushed down into the **mantle**.

THE OLDEST ROCKS AND MINERALS

Because of the rock cycle, there are no known rocks or minerals left from when the Earth first formed about 4.54 billion years ago.

The oldest rock discovered so far is gneiss rock from near the Acasta River in Canada—it's thought to be 3.96 billion years old.

The oldest mineral is zircon found in Australia's Jack Hills, dated at 4.4 billion years old!

10 When volcanoes erupt, hot, melted rock, or lava, comes out of the Earth. Lava cools and hardens, becoming new igneous rock.

9 Under the ground, squeezing and heating create metamorphic rock.

7 Other rock gets pushed upward, forming mountains.

8 Deep inside the Earth, rock gets hot and melts.

UNDERGROUND WORLD

The rock beneath our feet is not always solid. In many places, it contains cave chambers, hollows, tunnels, and underground rivers.

DISSOLVING AWAY

Most caves form in a type of rock called limestone, which is found in many parts of the world. As rain falls, it dissolves some carbon dioxide gas from the air, and more carbon dioxide as it soaks through the soil. This makes it into a very weak, watery acid. This acidic water gradually dissolves and eats away at limestone rock under the ground.

CAVE-FILLED LANDS

Over thousands or millions of years, this carves out deep underground chambers and passageways. Areas with lots of limestone are often filled with caves and holes in the ground. Earth scientists call this a "**karst**" landscape.

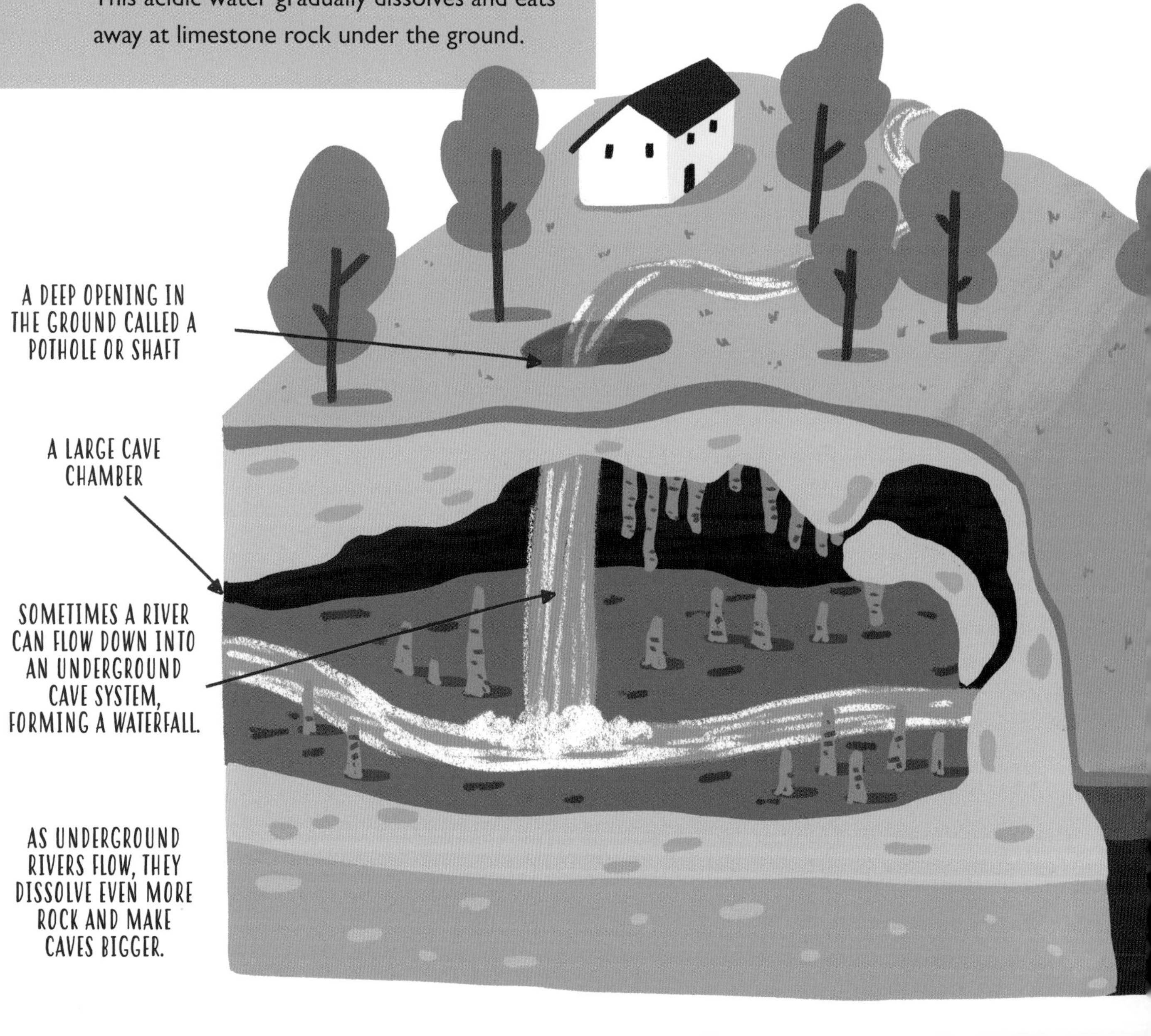

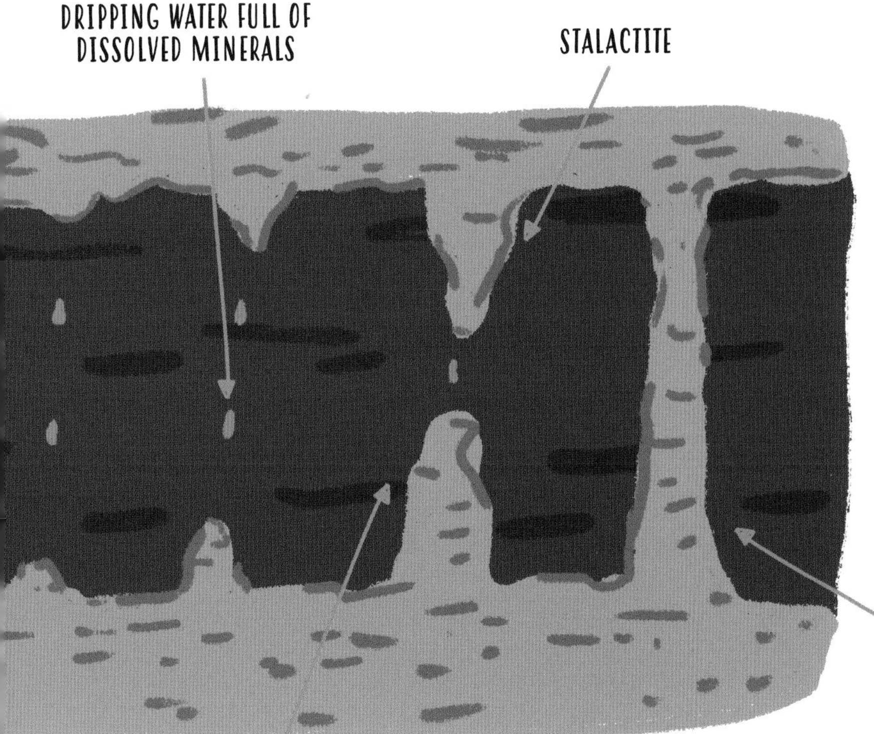

GOING UNDERGROUND

Humans have explored and mapped cave systems all over the planet. They sometimes have huge, interconnected networks of tunnels that extend for hundreds of kilometers.

STALACTITES AND STALAGMITES

In many caves, water filled with dissolved limestone rock drips from the ceiling. Each drop leaves a tiny bit of limestone on the ceiling, and a little bit more where it lands on the floor.

Over time, this creates limestone shapes that hang down from the ceiling, called stalactites, and pillars that rise up from the ground, called stalagmites.

OUT OF CURIOSITY

The deepest cave discovered so far is the Veryovkina Cave in Georgia, Eastern Europe. It's 2,212 m (7,257 ft) from the entrance to the deepest part.

AFTER FLOWING UNDERGROUND FOR AWHILE, THE RIVER EMERGES SOMEWHERE ELSE.

EARTHQUAKES AND VOLCANOES

Most of the time, the Earth's rocks and tectonic plates move verrrry slowly—so slowly that we don't notice. But in some places, they can go through sudden and dramatic changes when volcanoes erupt or earthquakes strike.

WHAT IS AN EARTHQUAKE?

During an earthquake, the ground suddenly moves, shakes, or ripples up and down. This is often a disaster, since strong earthquakes can cause buildings to fall down and open huge cracks in the ground. Earthquakes can also cause landslides, where soil or mud slips down a hill, burying people, homes, and cars.

HOW EARTHQUAKES HAPPEN

Earthquakes happen at plate boundaries, where the edges of the Earth's tectonic plates meet. As the plates gradually move and shift around, the edges can get caught on each other and become stuck. This builds up pressure, until suddenly, the plates slip.

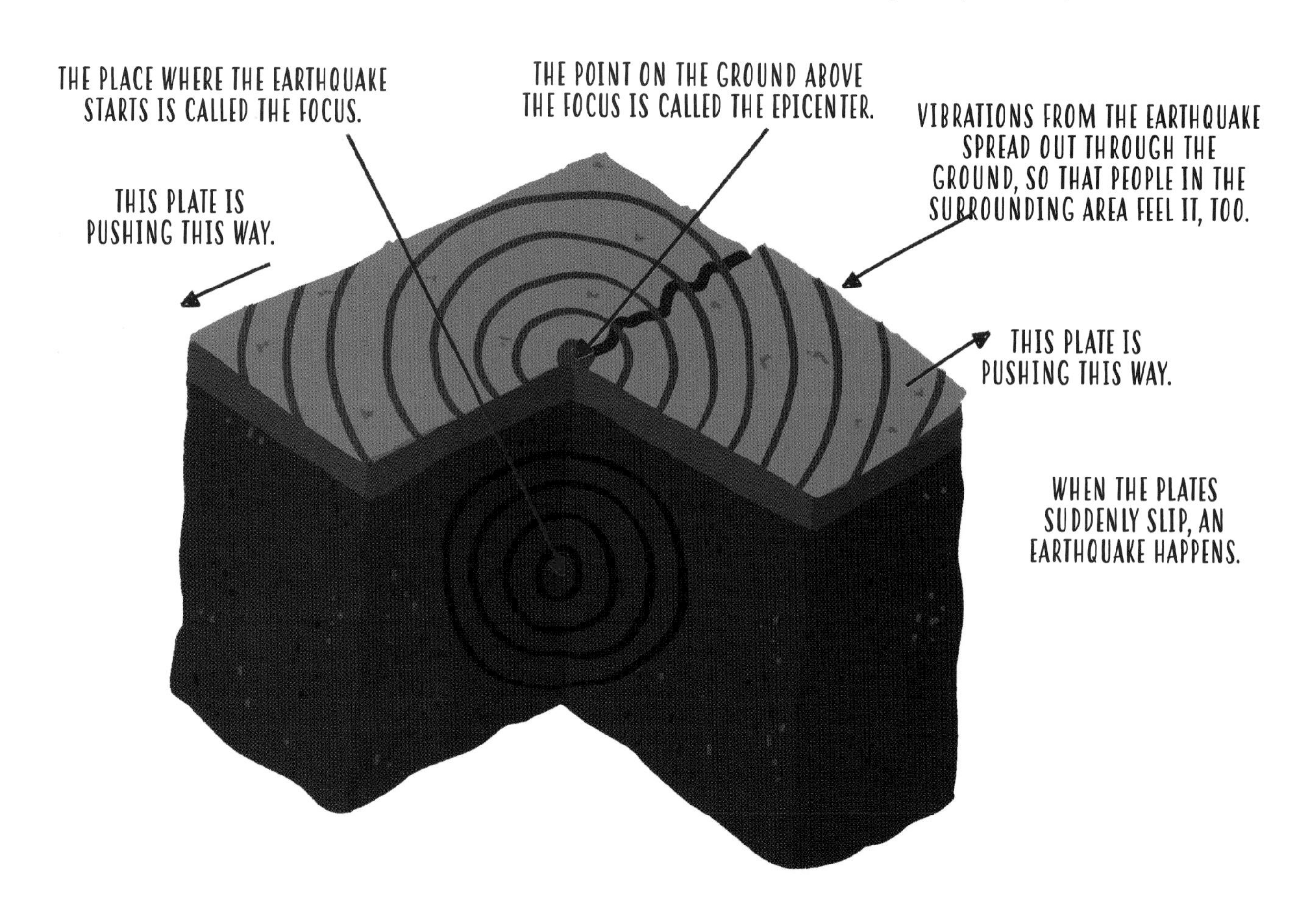

VIOLENT VOLCANOES

A volcano is a place where hot, molten rock from inside the Earth can escape through a crack or vent in the crust. When this happens, it's called a volcanic eruption. The red-hot melted rock that flows out is called lava.

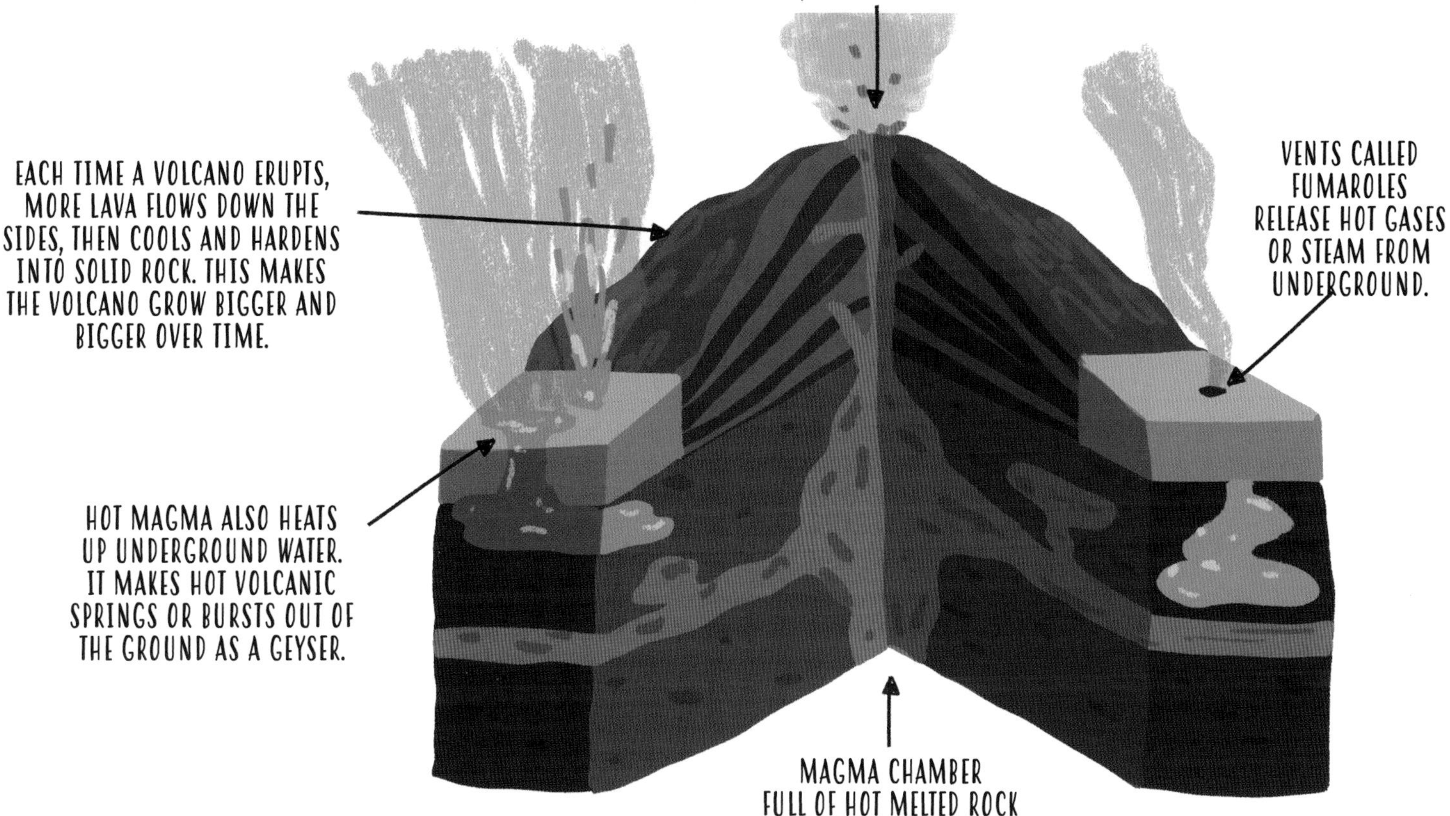

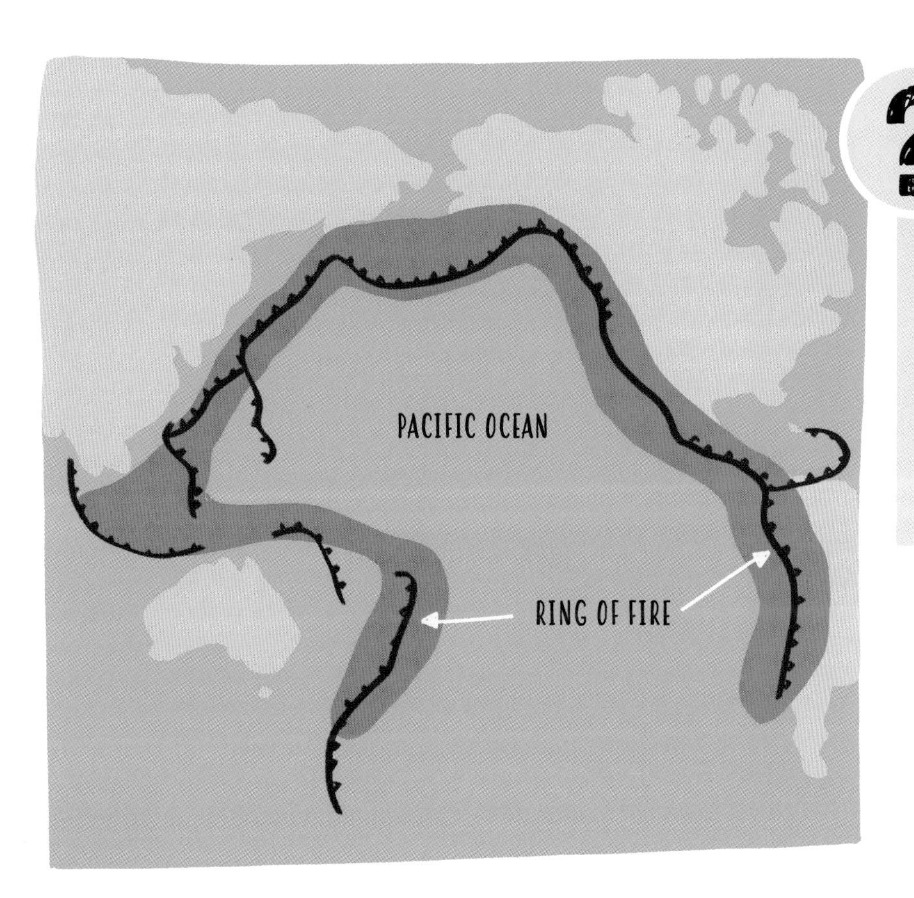

OUT OF CURIOSITY

Earthquakes and volcanoes are especially common around the "Ring of Fire." This is a giant circle of plate boundaries surrounding most of the Pacific Ocean.

GEOLOGICAL TIME

Geological time, or "deep time," is the history of the Earth since it first formed. It's a much, much longer time than our own human history, and it goes back billions of years.

THE DEEPER, THE OLDER

Sedimentary rocks (see page 19) collect in layers. We can still see these layers, called strata, in sedimentary rocks around the world. Since the deepest layers are the ones that formed the earliest, scientists can use them to calculate how old rocks are. This also applies to fossils found in the rocks.

DIPLODOCUS

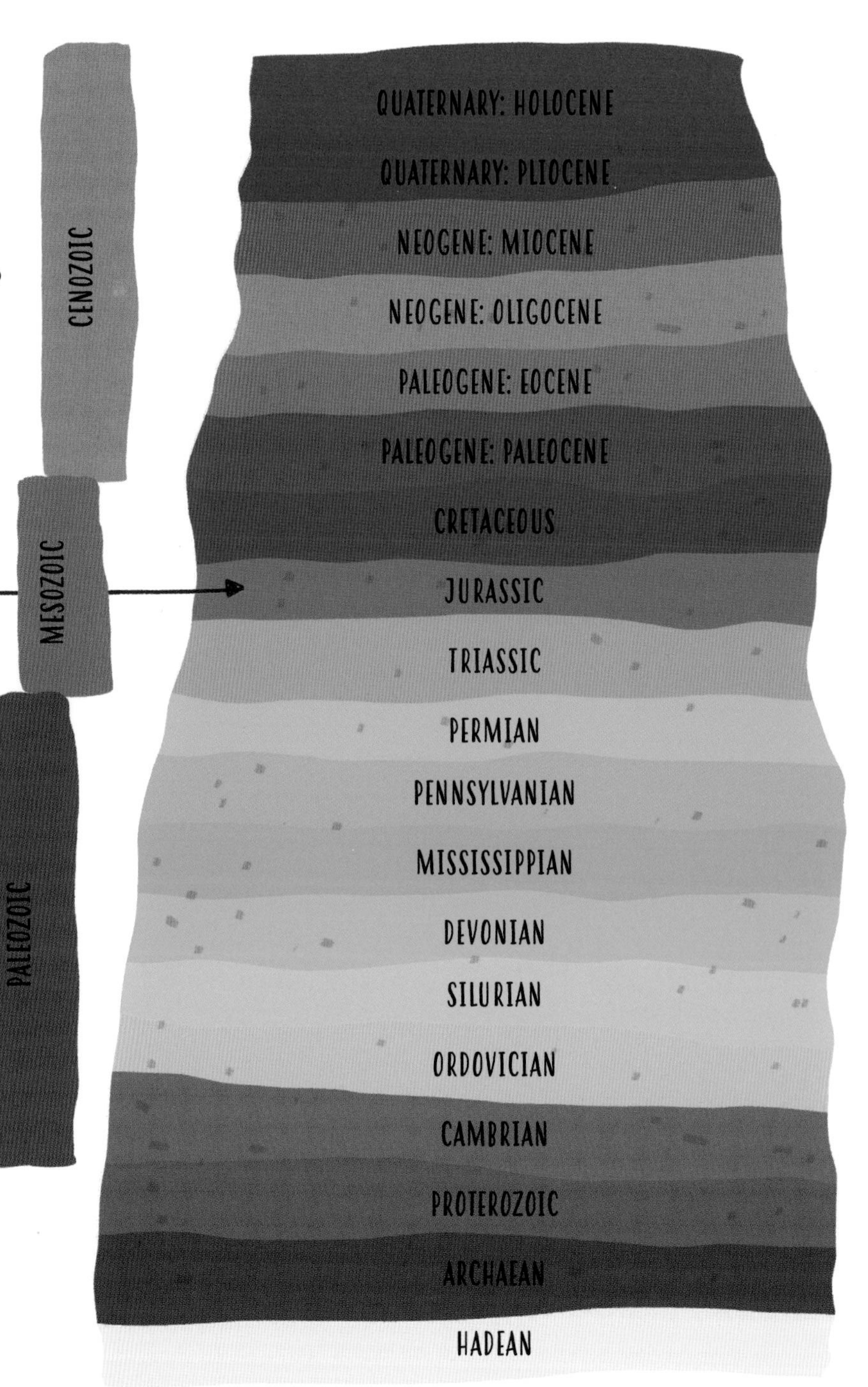

Scientists divide geological time into many smaller sections of time, known as eons, eras, periods, and epochs. This makes it easier to talk about when things happened.

For example, fossils show that the dinosaur *Diplodocus* lived in the Jurassic period, in the Mesozoic era.

IN THE 1780S, GEOLOGIST JAMES HUTTON STUDIED ROCKS AND SAW THAT THEY FORMED AND CHANGED VERY SLOWLY. HE REALIZED THAT THIS MEANT THAT THE EARTH MUST BE VERY OLD.

HOW OLD IS THE EARTH?

For a long time, no one really knew the age of the Earth. Some people thought it was just a few thousand years old. But from the 1700s onward, scientists realized that it was much older, by studying how rocks form, the rock cycle (see page 20), and rock strata.

DEEP TIME CLOCK

It's hard to imagine how long deep time is, but it can help to think of it as a clock showing the 24 hours in a day.

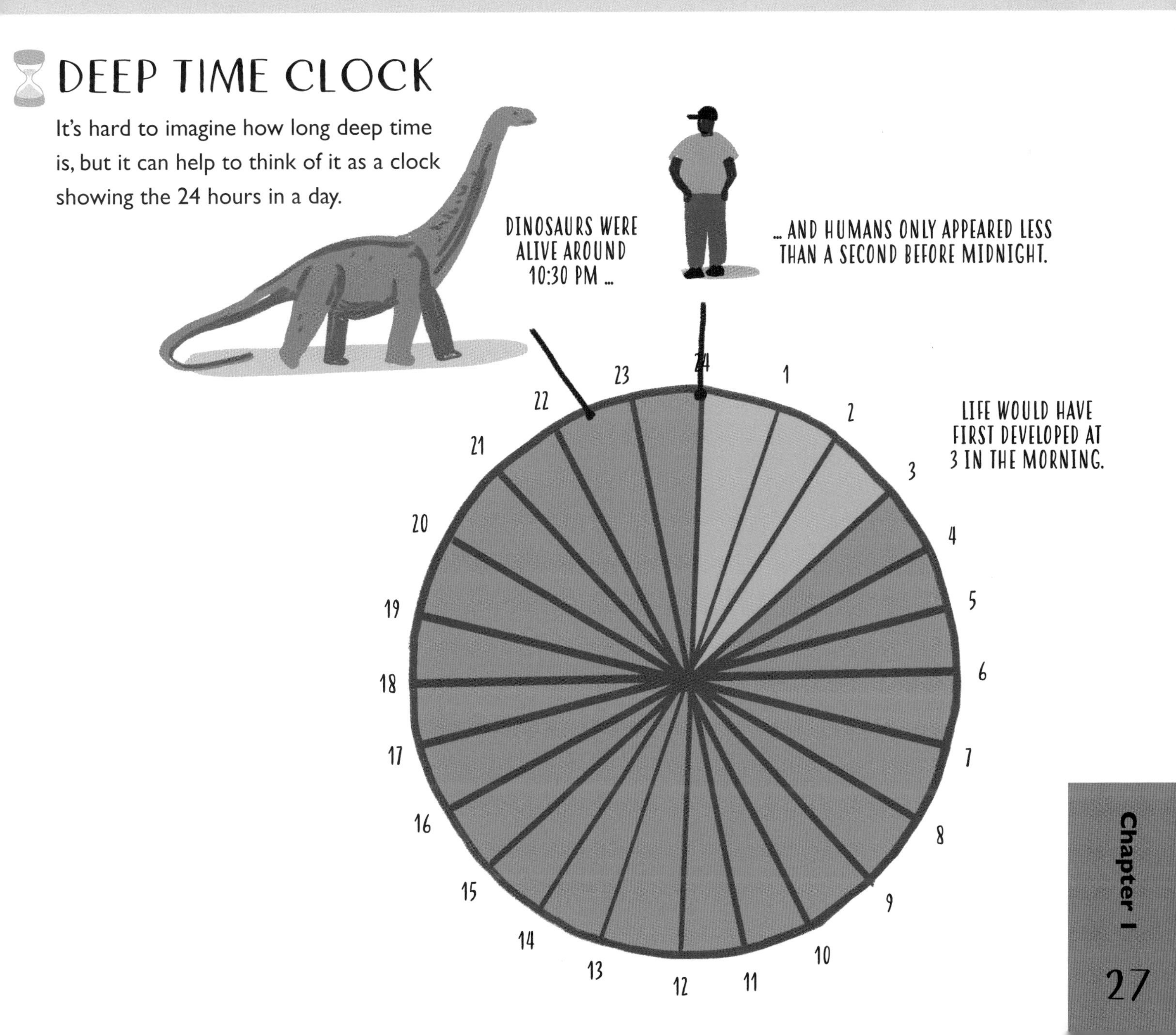

CHAPTER 2

WATER WORLD

About 71 percent, or almost three-quarters, of our planet is covered in seas and oceans. There's water on land, too, in ponds, lakes, and rivers, in rocks and soil, frozen into ice on high mountains, and around the poles. Even the air is full of water! It makes the clouds, rain, and snow. Water is vital to life on Earth, as plants, animals, and all other living things need it to survive.

In this chapter, we'll discover how water shapes landscapes, forms huge, powerful waves, and moves around in an endless cycle. And where did all this water come from in the first place? Read on to find out!

WHERE WATER CAME FROM

The Earth has had water on it for most of its history—probably around 4 billion years. It collected gradually over time to create the watery world that we know today.

WATER FROM SPACE

When the Solar System was still forming, millions of comets and asteroids crashed into the young Planet Earth. Comets are partly made of ice, and asteroids often contain hydrogen and oxygen, the ingredients that make up water. So, when they landed, they added more and more water to the Earth's surface.

WATER FROM INSIDE THE EARTH

However, this can't explain where all the water came from. Scientists think that some of it came from rocks inside the Earth, which also contain hydrogen and oxygen. When volcanoes erupt, they often pour out water in the form of steam, as well as lava, ash, and rock. The steam **condenses**, or turns into liquid water, as it cools. Early in the Earth's history, there were a lot more volcanic eruptions than there are today, giving us lots of extra water.

HOW MUCH WATER IS THERE?

If you stand on a beach and look out at the ocean, it looks like a mind-bogglingly huge amount of water. And it is! All the water in all the world's seas and oceans adds up to about 1,338 million cubic km (that's a cube that's 1 km long on each side), or 321 million cubic miles.

That's more than a trillion (1,000,000,000,000) public swimming pools, or about 7,000 trillion bathtubs full of water!

If you include the water on the land and in the atmosphere, and all the water that's frozen into ice, there's even more: 1,386 million cubic km (333 million cubic miles).

WATER IN A BALL

However, even though water covers most of the world, it's only a thin layer compared to the size of the planet. If all the water could be collected into a ball and put next to the Earth, it would look surprisingly small—like this (left)!

THE WATER CYCLE

The Earth's water doesn't stay still. It's constantly changing and moving around in a giant cycle called the water cycle. As it moves, it often changes state, too, between liquid water, gas in the air, and solid ice.

This picture on the right shows a simple version of the water cycle. In real life, this is happening all over the world in all kinds of different places. Some water is moving quickly, but some can spend many years stored in underground rocks or frozen into ice.

Water vapor, or gas, rises high into the sky. Higher up, the air is cooler. This makes the water vapor condense, or turn back into liquid. Tiny drops of liquid water form white, fluffy-looking clouds.

At the surface of seas, lakes, and rivers, some water evaporates. Water molecules break away and become water gas, or water vapor, in the air. The warmer the water is, the faster it evaporates.

At any one time, most of the world's water is in the seas and oceans.

The states of matter are the three main states that things can exist in: solid, liquid, and gas. For water, they are:

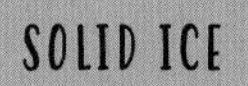

LIQUID WATER

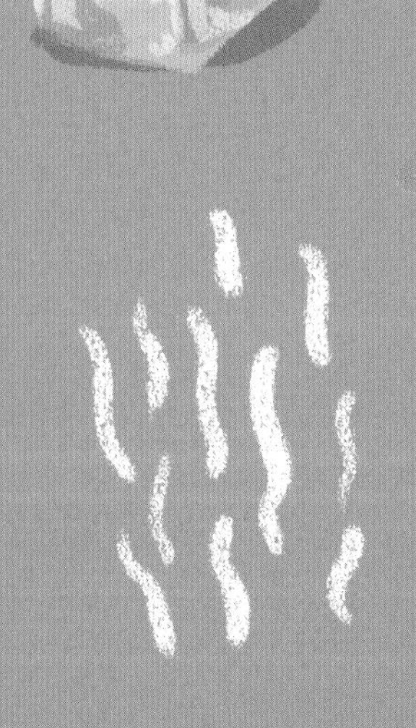

WATER VAPOR (OR GAS)

Wind often blows clouds over the land. In colder air, the water droplets join together and form raindrops, then fall as rain showers.

When clouds blow up over high mountains, the air is very cold, and they drop most of their rain.

Sometimes, it's so cold that the water in the clouds freezes and falls as snow.

Water is also held inside living things, such as trees and animals. Trees release water into the air from their leaves, and animals release water in their breath.

Rain and melted snow flow downhill, forming streams and rivers.

Most rivers eventually flow back into the sea or sometimes into large lakes or swamps.

Some water soaks into the soil and into underground rocks.

WATER IN THE GROUND

You might not hear much about groundwater, but it's very important. Most of the world's fresh (meaning non-salty) liquid water is in the ground. It's soaked into rocks and soil, and it's the reason we have wells!

THE WATER TABLE

Some water flows over the surface of the Earth in rivers and streams, but some soaks down into the ground. Just like water in the sea or in a lake, gravity pulls it down, so that it fills up the underground rocks to a flat level. This underground level, the upper surface of the water underground, is called the water table. The water table can rise and fall, depending on how much rain there is.

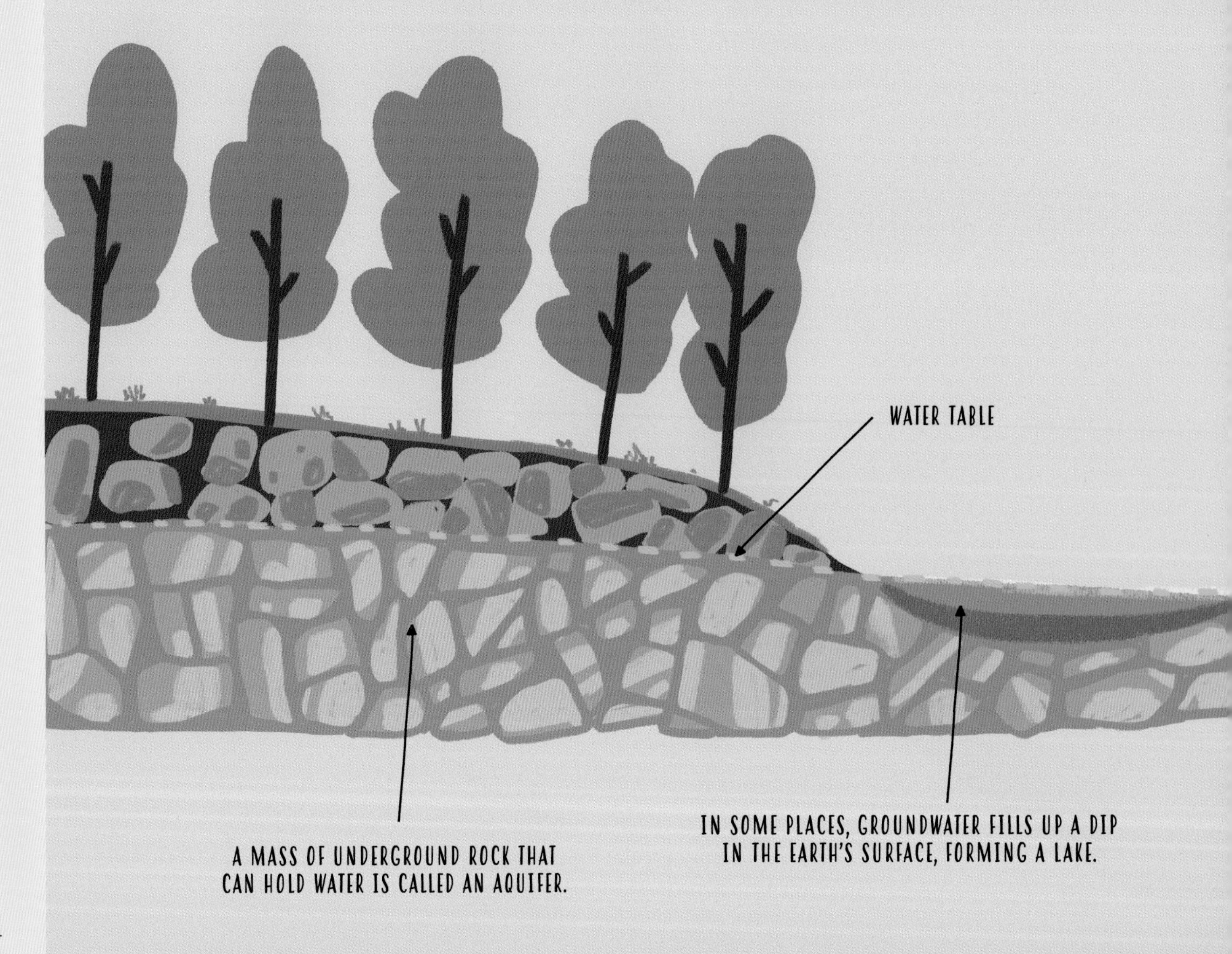

SPRING WATER

A spring is a place where **groundwater** naturally flows out of the ground. Springs can form where there's a layer of **porous** rock on top of a layer of nonporous rock. The water can't soak down any farther, so it starts to flow along sideways. If it reaches a valley or hillside, it can emerge as a spring.

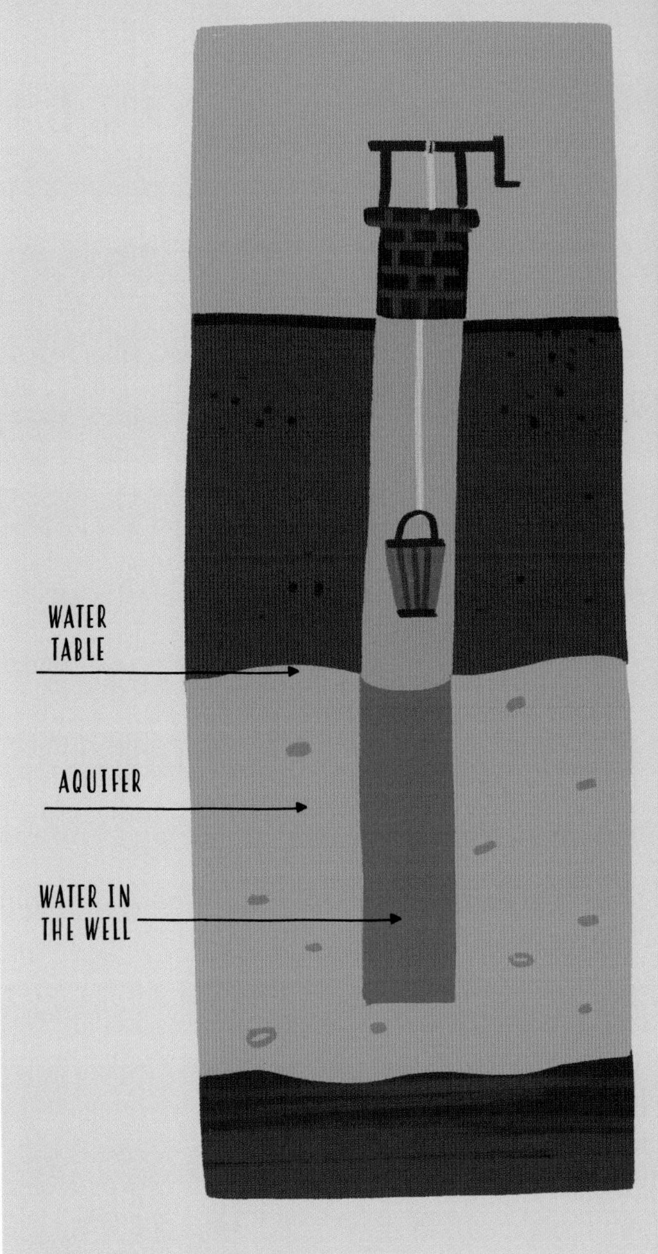

THE RIGHT KIND OF ROCK

Not all rocks can hold a store of water—only some types can.

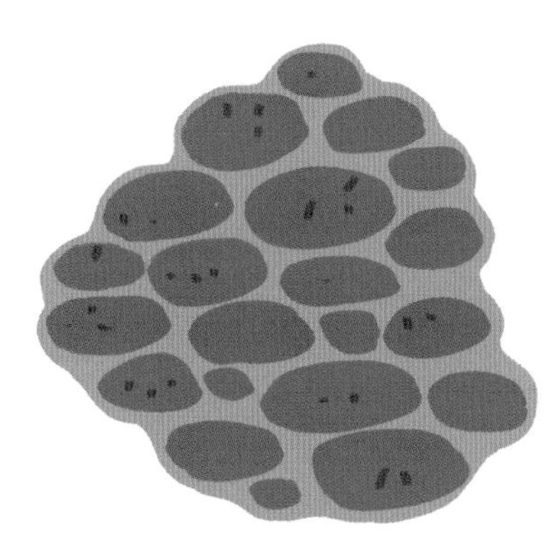

Porous rocks, such as sandstone and chalk, are made of tiny grains with spaces between them, so water can soak in.

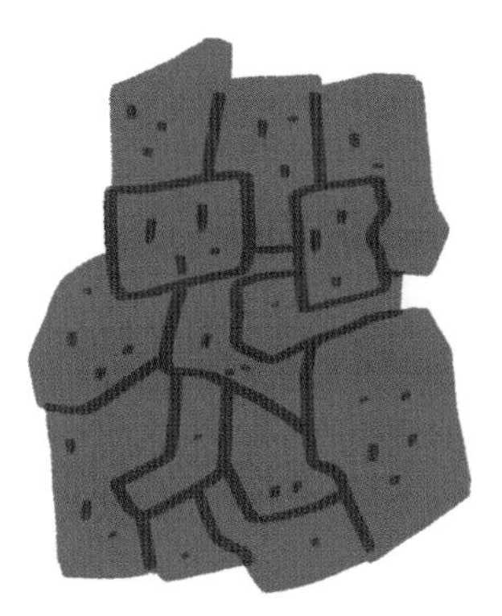

Nonporous rocks, such as granite and marble, are made of interlocking grains. They have very little space in between, so these rocks don't soak up much water.

DOWN THE WELL!

A well is a hole in the ground for collecting groundwater. It reaches down into an **aquifer**, making a space where groundwater collects. In a basic well, you just lower a bucket to collect the water. Modern wells often have pumps instead, which pump the water up to the surface and out of a faucet or tap.

RIVERS AND LAKES

Rivers and lakes only hold a tiny fraction of the world's water, but they're vital to life on land. They provide fresh drinking and bathing water for animals and humans, and a habitat for all kinds of living things. We also use them for fishing and transportation.

RIVER SYSTEMS

Most rivers start off as tiny streams in mountain areas. As streams flow down into valleys, they join together, becoming bigger streams and then large rivers. If you look at a map of a river and its tributaries (the streams and rivers that flow into it), you'll see that it looks a little bit like a tree with a trunk and lots of smaller branches.

TO THE SEA

As rivers flow over flatter land, they become slower and wider. Near the sea, they can spread out into a triangle-shaped **delta** or a wide **estuary.**

STREAMS

RIVER

ESTUARY

RECORD-BREAKERS

The biggest rivers and lakes are enormous!

- The Amazon River in South America is the world's biggest river, carrying the greatest amount of water. At its widest point, during the rainy season, it can be up to 40 km (25 mi) across.

- The longest river is the Nile in Africa, stretching about 6,650 km (4,130 mi) from the mountains of central Africa to the Mediterranean Sea.

- And the biggest lake is the Caspian Sea (actually a lake) in central Asia. It's around 1,200 km (750 mi) long and roughly the size of Norway.

AMAZING LAKES

Most lakes contain fresh water, but some are salty, like the Dead Sea in Israel and Jordan. This lake is in a hot desert at about 430 m (1,412 ft) below sea level. Rivers flow into it, but not out. Instead, the water evaporates, leaving behind salt that has dissolved into the water from the rocks. It's at least five times saltier than the sea. The extra salt makes the water very dense and easy to float in.

OUT OF CURIOSITY

Earth's deepest lake is Lake Baikal in Russia. Its deepest point is 1,642 m (5,387 ft) below the surface—deep enough to hold the Burj Khalifa, the world's tallest building!

SEAS AND OCEANS

From any seashore in the world, you could get in a boat and sail to any other seashore. The seas and oceans are all connected, surrounding all the Earth's continents with water.

SEASHORE SHELF

Close to the shore, the sea is shallow. It gets deeper and deeper as you move away from the coast. This is because, over millions of years, mud, soil, and rock fall into the sea from the land or get carried into the sea by rivers. They collect and build up to form an underwater structure called the continental shelf.

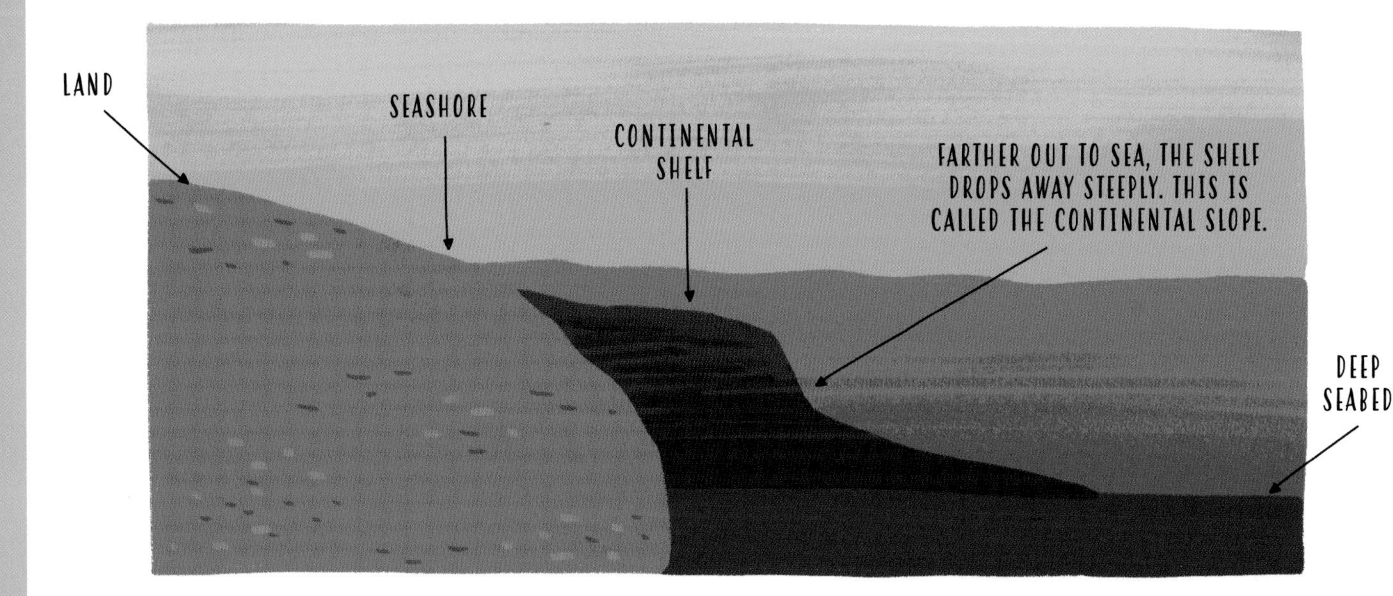

WHY IS THE SEA SALTY?

The sea is salty because as rain falls and rivers flow on land, they dissolve salt and other minerals from the rocks. They get carried into the sea. When water evaporates from the sea surface, it leaves the salt behind.

The sea tastes salty because it contains a lot of sodium chloride, the kind of salt we use in food.

PEOPLE COLLECT SEA SALT BY LEAVING SEAWATER TO EVAPORATE IN SHALLOW POOLS.

MAPPING THE SEABED

We can make maps of the seabed by measuring how deep the sea is in different places.

Long ago, people did this by lowering weights on ropes until they hit the bottom. Today, we often use **sonar**, which sends out pulses of sound, then measures how long they take to echo back. Some satellites can also measure the depth of the sea.

THIS SEABED MAP SHOWS PART OF THE INDIAN OCEAN.

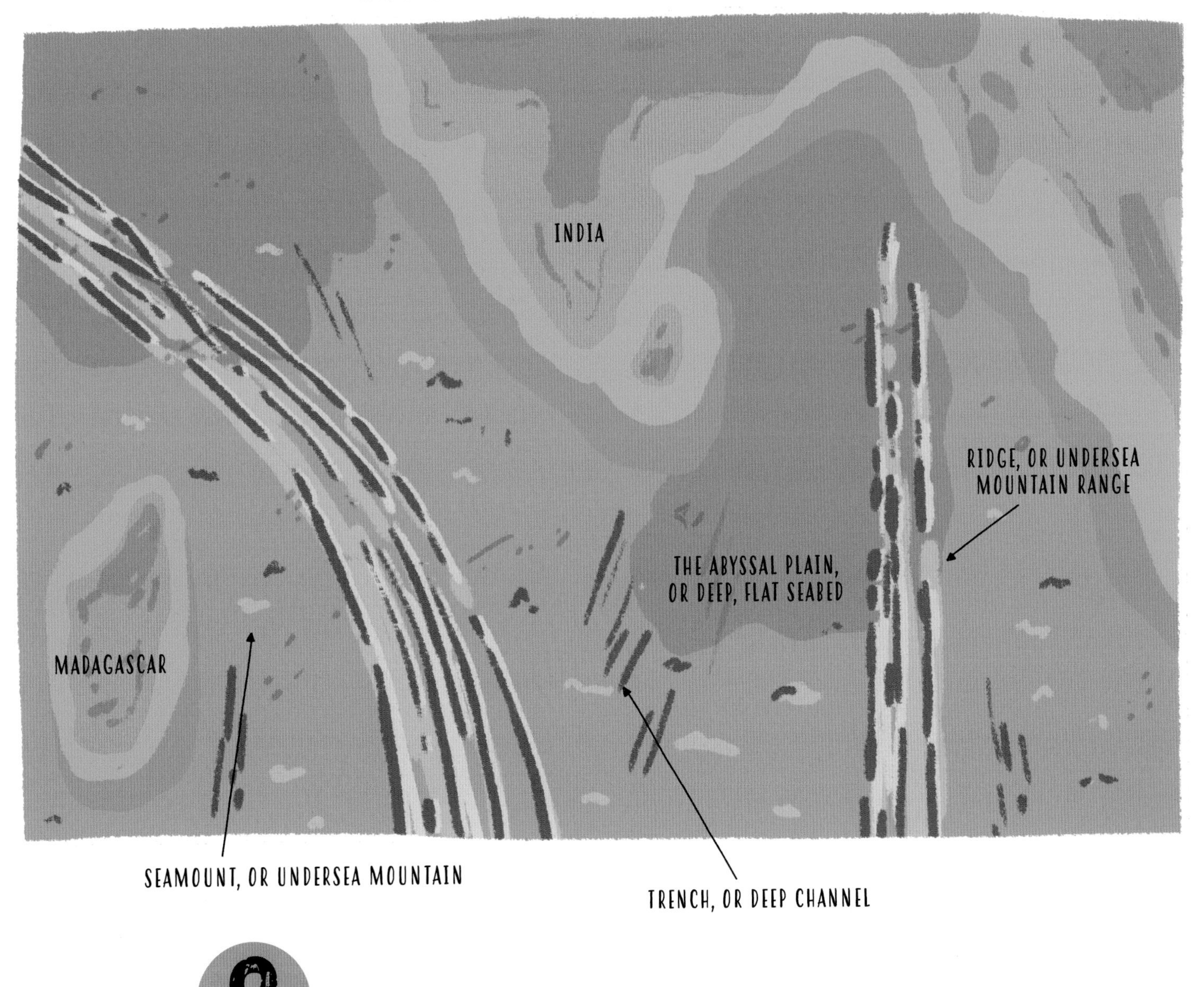

OUT OF CURIOSITY

Salt isn't the only mineral found in the sea. There are many other minerals in seawater too, including calcium, carbon, iron, and even tiny amounts of silver and gold.

OCEAN DEPTHS

The seas and oceans of the world vary in depth, from the shallow sunlit seabed to the deepest trenches way, way below the surface. Scientists divide them into several different zones.

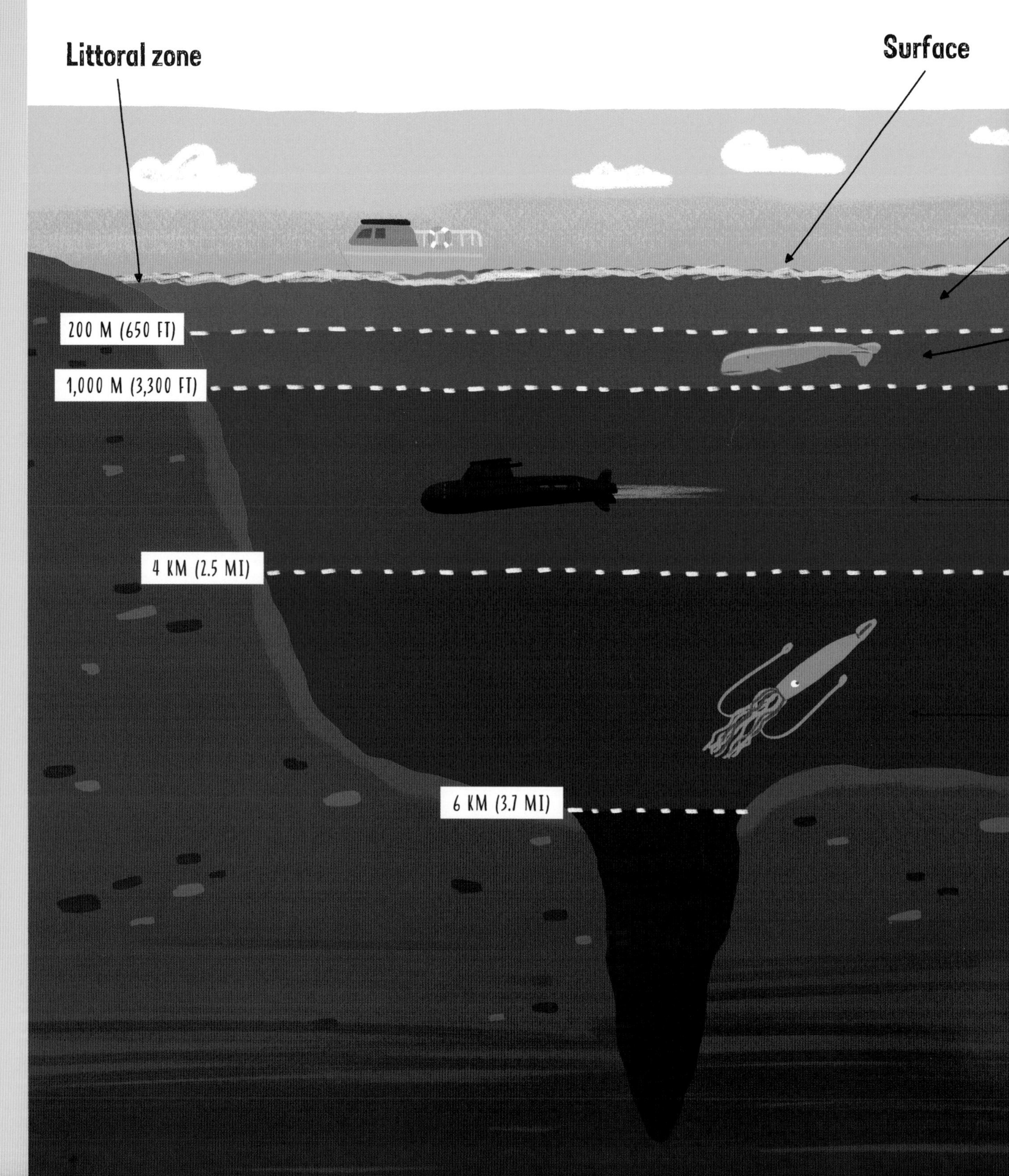

GOING DOWN...

When you stand on the beach, you're in the littoral zone. This is the shallow part of the sea on top of the **continental shelf.** It includes the seashore and part of the sea that's affected by tides and breaking waves.

The open ocean, away from the coast, is called the pelagic zone. It has five main depth zones:

Sunlight zone, also called the Epipelagic zone

Between the surface and 200 m (650 ft) down, this is the warmest and lightest zone. Sunlight can shine through the water, so plants and plankton live here, along with many other sea creatures.

Twilight or Mesopelagic zone

From 200 to 1,000 m down (650 to 3,300 ft), this zone is colder and darker than the Sunlight zone, but still gets a little sunlight. Lots of fish and deep-diving whales can be found here.

Midnight or Bathypelagic zone

Below 1,000 m (3,300 ft) deep, the ocean is completely dark, since sunlight cannot shine this far through the water. It's very cold, and there are fewer sea creatures. Many of them are bioluminescent, meaning that their bodies can light up.

Abyssal zone

The zone from 4,000 to 6,000 m (2.5 to 3.7 mi) includes large areas of deep seabed called the abyssal plain. It's dark and very cold, with huge water pressure.

Hadal zone

From 6,000 m (3.7 mi) down to the deepest parts of the seabed at the bottom of deep ocean trenches, this is one of the least-explored parts of Planet Earth—but some sea creatures do survive here.

HOT WATER

In some places, hot water from under the seabed pours out into the sea though openings called hydrothermal vents. The water is full of dissolved minerals. The minerals build up around the vents to form chimney shapes called black smokers.

OUT OF CURIOSITY

The water pressure in the Hadal zone is so great, it would crush a normal submarine. But we can explore the deepest depths in extra-strong deep-sea submersibles.

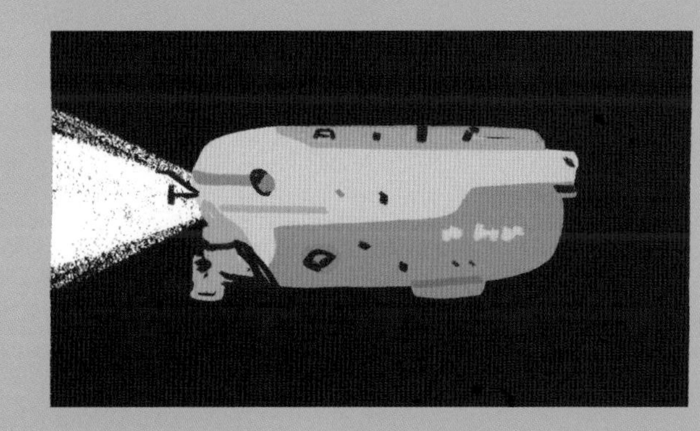

WAVES AND TSUNAMIS

Rivers, lakes, seas, and oceans are mostly made of liquid water, and liquids can flow, splash, and ripple. Waves are ripples and movements on the water's surface—and in the oceans, they can be huge!

WHAT MAKES WAVES?

Waves usually form as wind blows across water, pushing at its surface. You can see this happening if you blow gently across a glass of water—small waves will appear. In a vast area of water, like a sea or large lake, the wind keeps blowing on the waves, making them bigger and bigger. Ocean waves can sometimes be over 20 m (66 ft) high, as tall as a six-story building!

OUT AT SEA, OCEAN WAVES TRAVEL ACROSS THE SURFACE, MAKING THE WATER MOVE UP AND DOWN. BOATS AND SHIPS TILT AND SWAY AS THEY PASS OVER THEM.

SURFERS RIDE ON THE FRONT SLOPE OF A WAVE AS IT APPROACHES THE SHORE.

IN SHALLOWER WATER, WAVES ROLL OVER AND BREAK.

HOW WAVES BREAK

As waves reach shallower water, the bottom part of the wave drags on the bottom and slows down, while the top moves forward faster. This makes it curl forward and break.

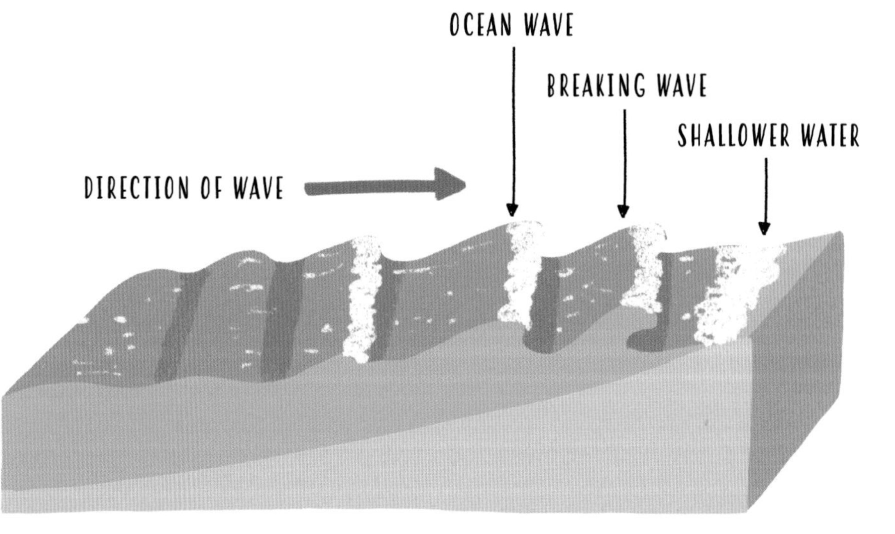

TSUNAMIS

Big waves carry a lot of energy and can be very dangerous. They can sink boats and sweep people away. This is especially true of **tsunamis**, the biggest waves of all.

Tsunamis are not caused by wind. Instead, they happen when a sudden movement makes the water shake suddenly. This creates an extra-large ripple that spreads out in all directions, like when a pebble is dropped into a pond. An earthquake on the seabed, a landslide falling into the sea, or a volcanic eruption close to the sea can all cause a tsunami.

1. A seabed earthquake makes the water in the sea move, causing a giant ripple.

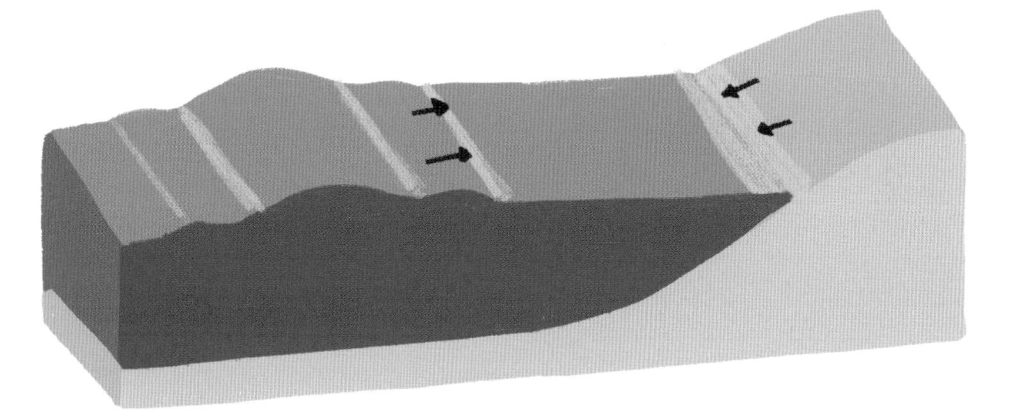

2. The wave is bigger and wider than a normal ocean wave. It travels very fast across the sea.

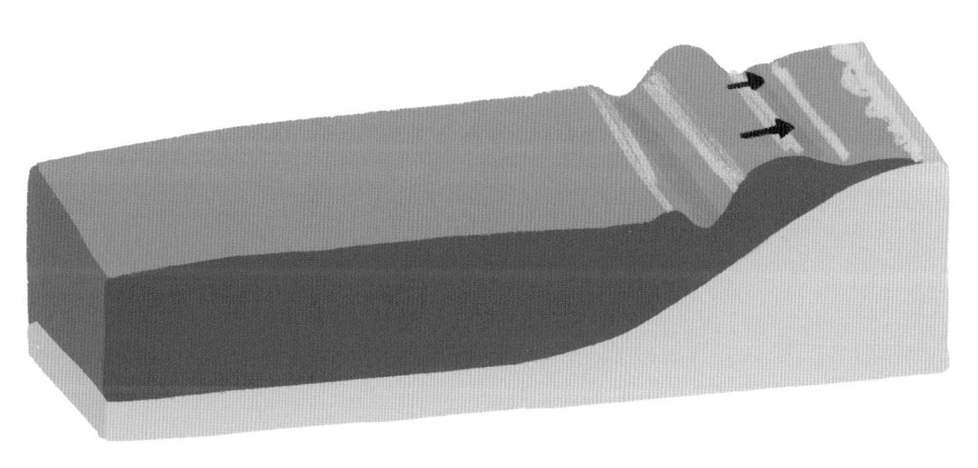

3. When it reaches the shore, the tsunami wave starts to slow down and pile up, becoming higher. It doesn't always break, but it can flow a long way onto the land, sweeping away people, vehicles, and buildings.

ICE AND GLACIERS

At 0°C (32°F) or below, liquid water freezes into solid ice. Some very cold places, such as the areas around the North and South Poles, high mountains, and mountain ranges, are covered with ice all year round.

ICE ZONES

On this map, you can see the parts of the world that are covered in ice. The biggest areas are the two ice sheets: huge, thick layers of ice that cover most of Antarctica and Greenland. Smaller ice-covered areas, usually on high mountains, are called ice caps. Most icy areas shrink in summer and expand in winter.

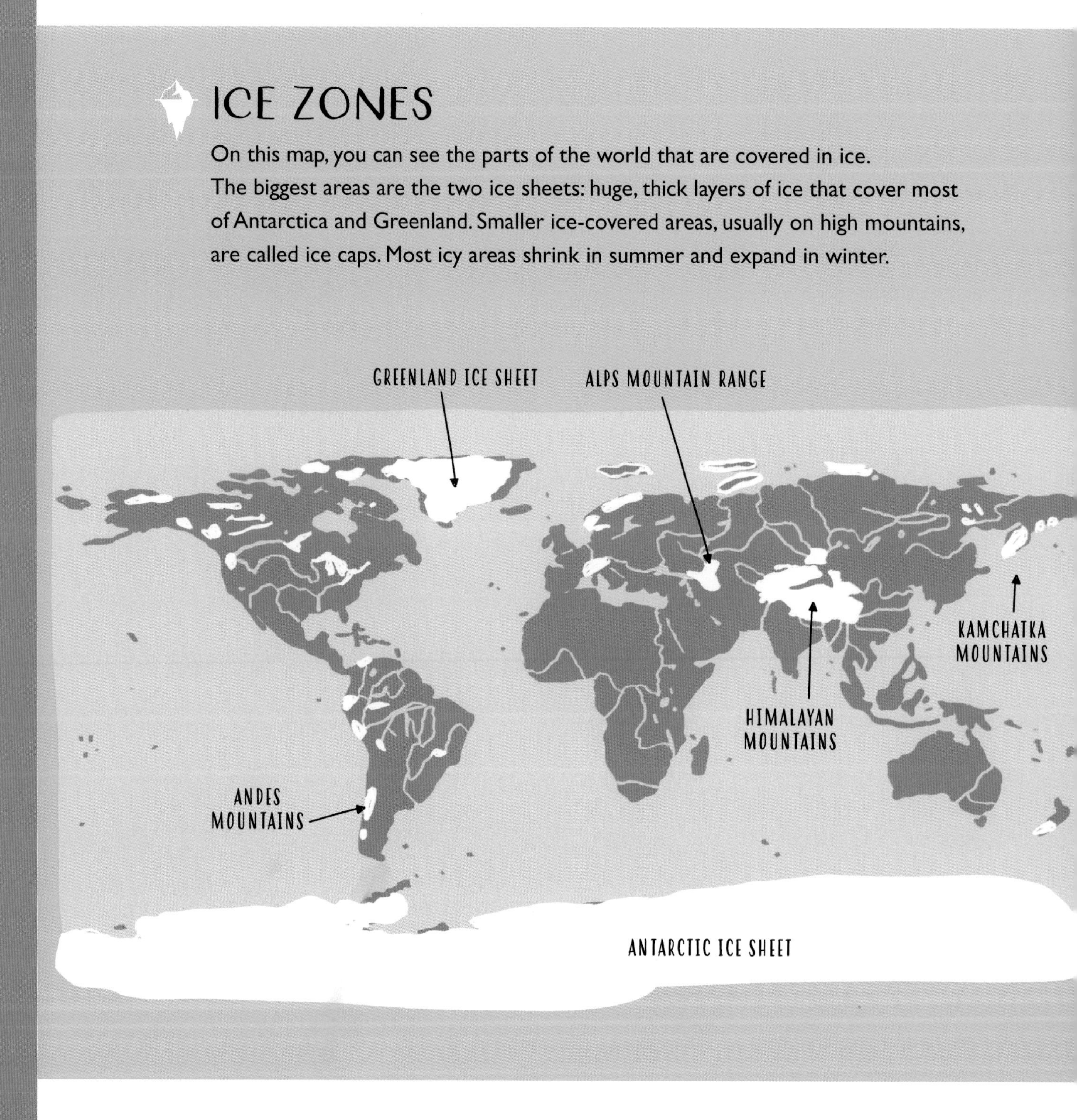

RIVERS OF ICE

A glacier is like a very big, slow river made of solid ice. When snow falls on an ice cap or ice sheet, it packs down into solid ice. Eventually, there's so much ice that it starts to move downhill under its own weight, flowing down a valley. Lower down, it's warmer, so the ice at the bottom end begins to melt. In some places, especially Antarctica, glaciers flow off the land and out over the sea.

Glaciers often crack as they move, and gaps called crevasses open up.

The front end of a glacier, where the ice is melting, is called the snout, toe, or terminus.

ICEBERGS

Icebergs are big, floating chunks of ice. They form when ice breaks off from a glacier or ice sheet that flows off the land and out into the sea. Icebergs range from the size of a large house up to the size of a small country! The biggest one ever measured was 295 km (185 mi) long and 37 km (21 mi) wide—about the same size as Jamaica. It was named B-15, and formed in March 2000.

Gradually, glaciers drift into warmer waters, break up, and melt away. Only 10 percent of a glacier can be seen above the surface. The rest is hidden underwater.

ISLANDS AND COASTS

Where the land meets the sea, the world has over 1,000,000 km (620,000 mi) of coastline. About three-quarters of the world's countries have a coastline. Even a small country can have a long coastline if it's very wiggly or has a lot of islands, like Norway.

NORWEGIAN SEA

NORWAY

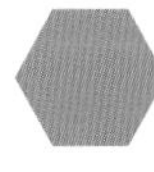

SHAPES OF THE SHORE

The coastline is always changing. Waves and tides wash sand and pebbles ashore, or they crash against rocks and cliffs and wear them away. Over time, the action of the sea creates different shapes, or landforms, along the shore.

1. A bay forms where waves have worn away softer rock.
2. A headland is made of harder, longer-lasting rock.
3. Cliffs form as waves wear away the shore, and the coastline slowly moves inland.
4. Waves can eat away under cliffs, too, creating a sea cave.
5. When crashing waves wear away the rock under a headland, an arch forms.
6. When an arch finally collapses, it leaves a stack standing alone out at sea.

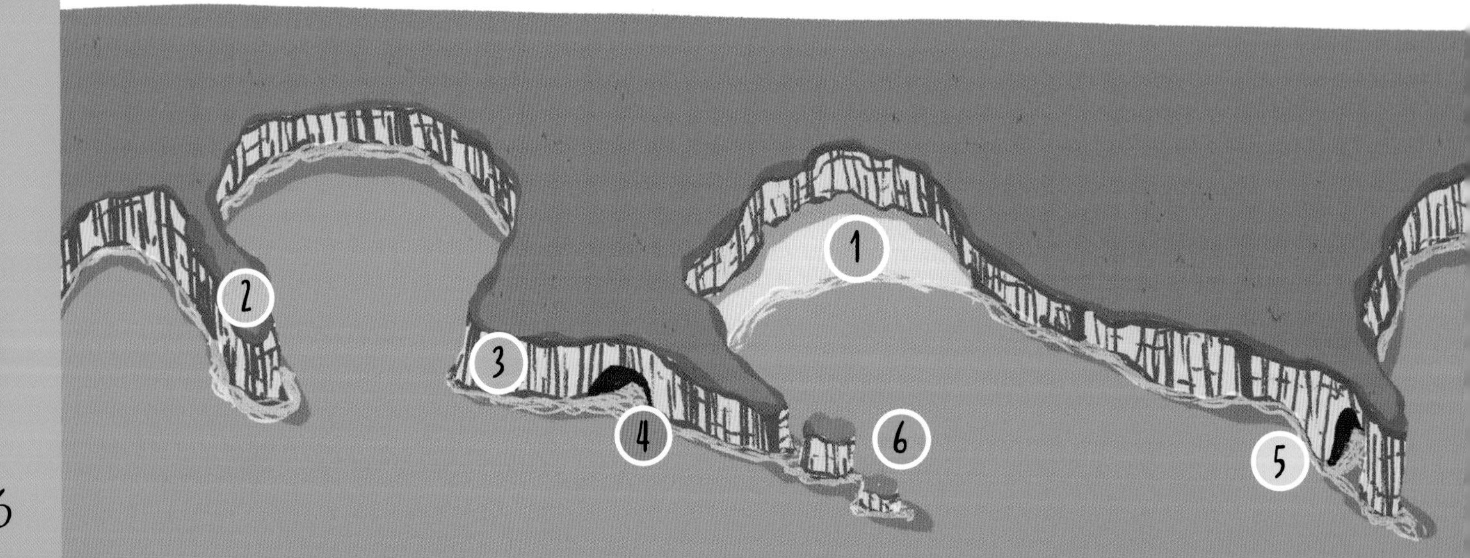

ISLANDS

Across the world there are thousands of islands surrounded by water in the world's lakes, rivers, seas, and oceans. They range from tiny remote rocks to enormous Greenland, the world's biggest island (apart from the continents themselves). Islands can stand alone, or in an island group or archipelago.

IN THE SEA, THERE ARE TWO MAIN TYPES OF ISLANDS:

Oceanic islands, such as Madeira, stand in the deep ocean. They are the tops of mountains or volcanoes rising from the seabed.

Continental islands are close to a continent and lie in the shallower water of the continental shelf.

WHAT MAKES A BEACH?

As rivers flow, they carry sand and pebbles along with them into the sea. In shallower coastal waters and sheltered bays, gentle waves wash sand and pebbles ashore, forming a beach.

A PLACE TO LIVE

The area between high tide and low tide is called the intertidal zone. It's washed by water twice a day as the tide ebbs and flows. It's home to seaweeds, crabs, worms that burrow under the sand, and limpets that cling to rocks. Some sea creatures stay safe in rock pools when the tide is out.

CHAPTER 3

THE ATMOSPHERE AND WEATHER

The atmosphere is a layer of gases surrounding the Earth, pulled close to the planet by gravity. The atmosphere gives us air to breathe, helps keep the planet warm, and makes the sky look blue. If it wasn't there, we wouldn't be able to survive at all.

However, it never stays still. Air, water, and heat held in the atmosphere are constantly moving and swirling around, giving us different types of weather. From welcome rain to fill rivers and water our crops, to powerful windstorms, blizzards, mighty floods, and even strange showers of fish, the weather plays a major part in our lives, as we'll see in this chapter.

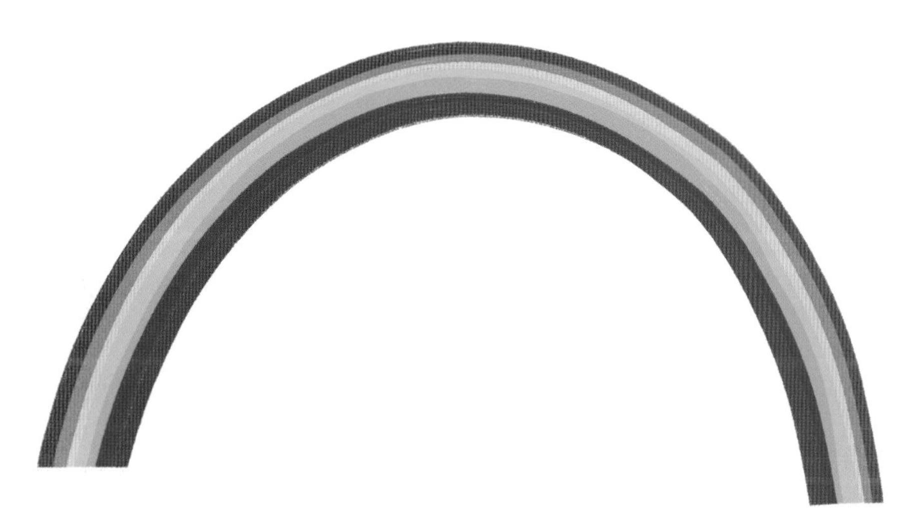

THE EARTH'S ATMOSPHERE

Viewed from space, the atmosphere looks like a thin, bluish skin around the planet. The farther away from the planet you go, the less atmosphere there is—until you're in outer space, where there's no atmosphere at all.

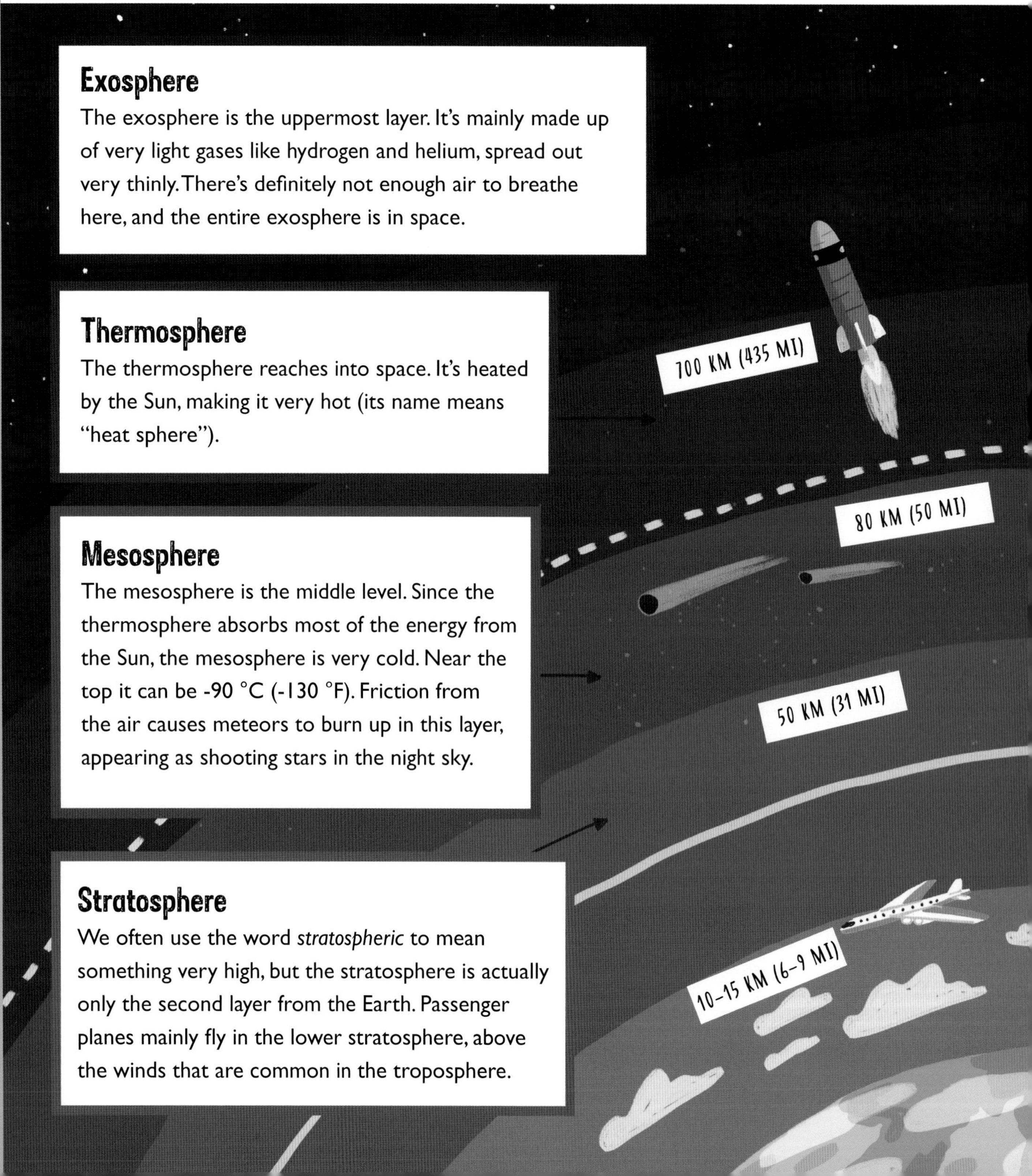

Exosphere

The exosphere is the uppermost layer. It's mainly made up of very light gases like hydrogen and helium, spread out very thinly. There's definitely not enough air to breathe here, and the entire exosphere is in space.

Thermosphere

The thermosphere reaches into space. It's heated by the Sun, making it very hot (its name means "heat sphere").

700 KM (435 MI)

80 KM (50 MI)

Mesosphere

The mesosphere is the middle level. Since the thermosphere absorbs most of the energy from the Sun, the mesosphere is very cold. Near the top it can be -90 °C (-130 °F). Friction from the air causes meteors to burn up in this layer, appearing as shooting stars in the night sky.

50 KM (31 MI)

Stratosphere

We often use the word *stratospheric* to mean something very high, but the stratosphere is actually only the second layer from the Earth. Passenger planes mainly fly in the lower stratosphere, above the winds that are common in the troposphere.

10–15 KM (6–9 MI)

LAYERS OF THE ATMOSPHERE

Like the oceans, scientists divide the atmosphere into several different layers. In this diagram, the atmosphere is shown much deeper than it really is, so that you can see all the layers clearly.

THE INGREDIENTS OF AIR

Most of the atmosphere, especially in the lower levels, is made of air. It's a mixture of gases, including oxygen, which we need to breathe in to help our cells to work. The main ingredients of air are:

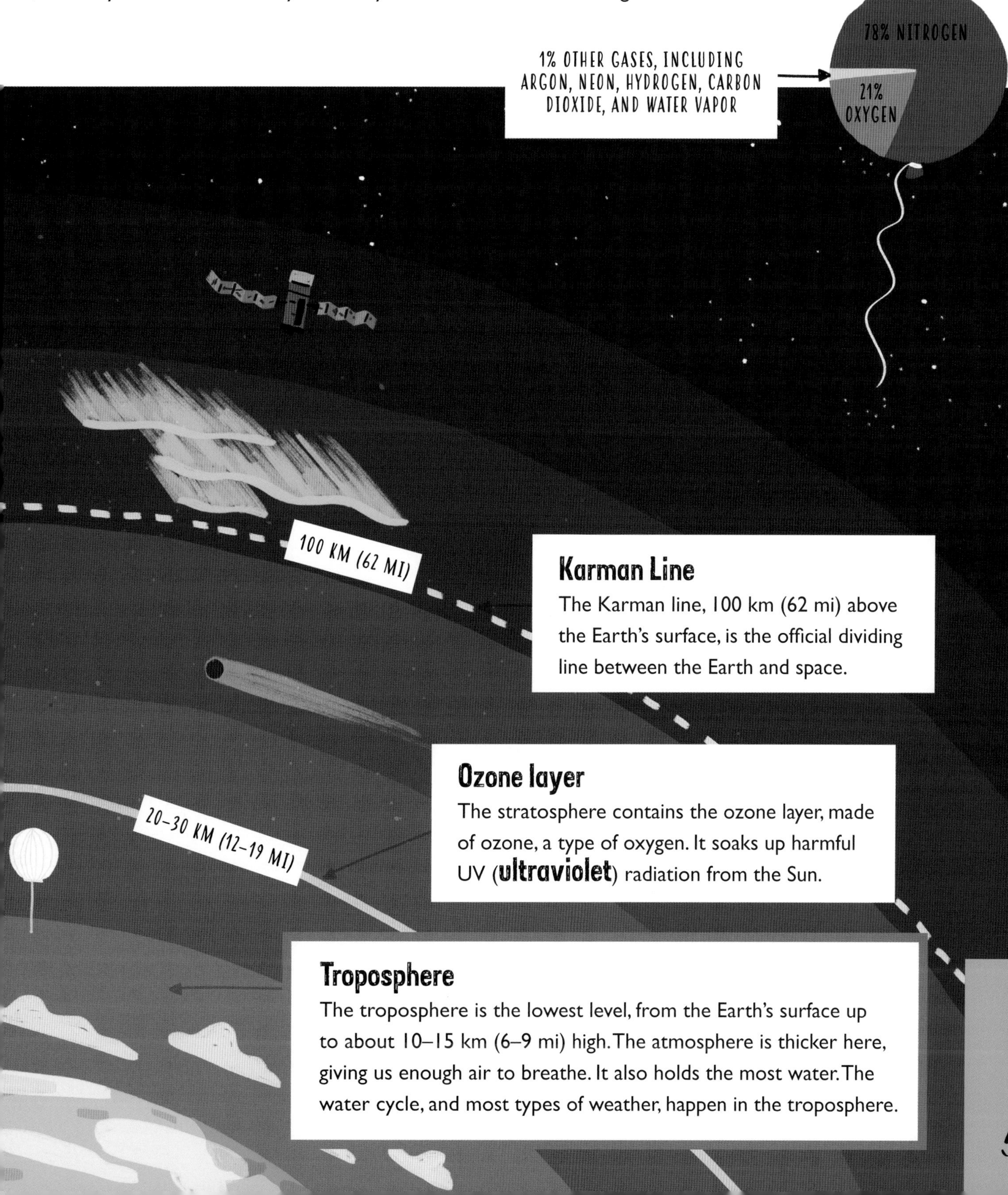

78% NITROGEN

1% OTHER GASES, INCLUDING ARGON, NEON, HYDROGEN, CARBON DIOXIDE, AND WATER VAPOR

21% OXYGEN

100 KM (62 MI)

Karman Line

The Karman line, 100 km (62 mi) above the Earth's surface, is the official dividing line between the Earth and space.

Ozone layer

The stratosphere contains the ozone layer, made of ozone, a type of oxygen. It soaks up harmful UV (**ultraviolet**) radiation from the Sun.

20–30 KM (12–19 MI)

Troposphere

The troposphere is the lowest level, from the Earth's surface up to about 10–15 km (6–9 mi) high. The atmosphere is thicker here, giving us enough air to breathe. It also holds the most water. The water cycle, and most types of weather, happen in the troposphere.

WEATHER AND CLIMATE

Everywhere in the world has weather! Air, water, and heat from the Sun are constantly changing and moving around in the atmosphere, creating wind, rain, snow, storms, or warm, sunny days. Each part of the world also has its own climate or typical weather patterns.

WHAT'S THE DIFFERENCE?

Weather and climate are related, but they are not the same thing.

• Weather can change from day to day—or even from one minute to the next. When you step outside, it could be hot or cold, rainy, cloudy, very windy, or snowing.

• Climate means the typical weather patterns in a particular place. For example, deserts are places with a very dry climate. They have hardly any rain or clouds and are often very hot during the day and colder at night.

ON A SINGLE DAY, THE WEATHER COULD BE CLOUDY AND RAINY, FOLLOWED BY A THUNDERSTORM WITH LIGHTNING. LATER, AFTER THE STORM CLOUDS HAVE CLEARED, IT MIGHT BE SUNNY AND WARM FOR A TIME, WITH A RAINBOW IN THE SKY.

CLIMATE ZONES

Different parts of the world have different climates. For example, areas close to the equator get more of the Sun's heat and light energy than areas around the poles, so they have warmer climates. This map shows the main climate zones.

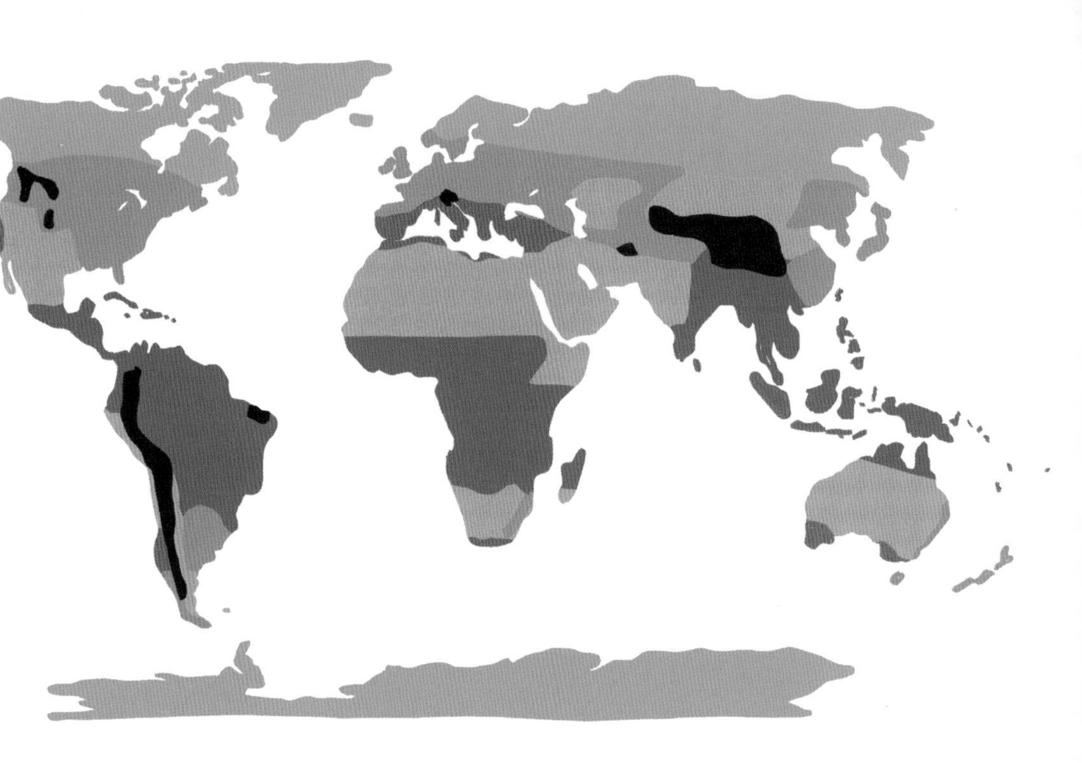

- POLAR: COLD, ICY CLIMATE WITH LONG, DARK WINTERS
- TEMPERATE: MEDIUM CLIMATE WITH A MIXTURE OF WEATHER
- ARID: DRY OR DESERT CLIMATES
- TROPICAL: HOT, HUMID, AND RAINY CLIMATE CLOSE TO THE EQUATOR
- MEDITERRANEAN: HOT, DRY SUMMERS AND COOL, WET WINTERS
- MOUNTAIN: COLD, WINDY, FOGGY, AND SNOWY

LOCAL CLIMATES

Within the main climate zones, places can have their own local climates.

Mountains in South America's Atacama desert have a cool, dry, but often foggy climate.

Taiga, or snow forest, is a type of evergreen forest around the Arctic. It has a cold climate with snowy winters and short summers.

THE POWER OF THE SUN

Most weather happens because of the Sun. As it shines, it radiates heat energy. This heats the air, and makes water evaporate from the sea. Light from the Sun plays a part in the weather too.

WARMED BY THE SUN

The Sun glows with normal light that we can see, but also with invisible UV (**ultraviolet**) and IR (**infrared**) light. Like visible light, infrared light travels through space in the form of energy waves. When they hit the Earth, they make it heat up. The same thing happens when the Sun shines on you, and you can feel yourself getting warmer.

HEAT FROM THE SUN

HEAT FROM THE EARTH

HEAT AND AIR

When the ground is warm, it heats up the air above it. Warmer air is lighter than colder air, so this warmed air rises upwards, making the air around it move too.

HEAT AND WATER

When sunlight hits the sea, it warms the surface and helps it to evaporate faster. This adds water vapor to the air, which can eventually become rain or snow.

So the Sun powers the weather, making air, water, and heat energy constantly move around.

WHAT MAKES A RAINBOW?

A rainbow is one of the most beautiful of all weather sights. Long ago, people often thought rainbows must be magical. In fact, they happen when sunlight shines in and out of falling raindrops.

Visible sunlight is made up of different **wavelengths** of light. Each wavelength has its own color. When they're all mixed together, they look white.

But as sunlight shines into a raindrop, it bends, or refracts, as it passes from the air into the water. This makes the light split into different wavelengths and colored bands.

The light reflects off the inside of the raindrop and back toward the Sun. As it leaves the raindrop, it refracts again, bending even more.

WHAT YOU SEE

When you're looking at lots of raindrops with the Sun behind you, each drop shines a different shade back toward you, depending on the angle you see it from. Together, this makes a curved rainbow appear.

OUT OF CURIOSITY

Rainbows are actually circular! You usually only see a half-circle because the ground is in the way. But you can sometimes see a whole-circle rainbow from a plane.

CLOUDS

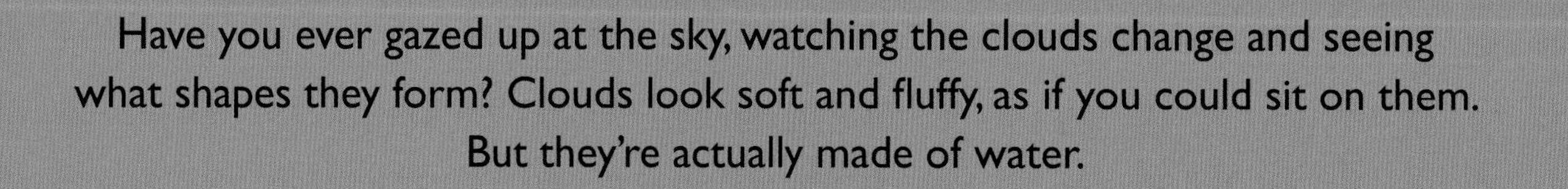

Have you ever gazed up at the sky, watching the clouds change and seeing what shapes they form? Clouds look soft and fluffy, as if you could sit on them. But they're actually made of water.

WHERE CLOUDS COME FROM

First, water evaporates into the air from seas and lakes, turning into water vapor, or gas. Water vapor also comes from trees, other plants, and animals.

High in the sky, it's colder, and this makes water vapor condense, or turn back into liquid. It's easiest for water to condense onto a cold surface, so it usually condenses around tiny specks of dust in the air, forming tiny, floating water drops.

Lots of small water drops together form clouds. They usually look white, because the tiny drops reflect lots of light. If they are blocking the sunlight, they look dark.

TYPES OF CLOUDS

There are many different types of clouds, with different shapes, patterns, and textures. The temperature, wind, and altitude (how high they are) affect how clouds look. Here are some of the cloud types you could spot in the sky and what their names mean:

Cirrus
(which means "hair")
Light, wispy, high-up clouds made of tiny ice crystals.

Cirrocumulus ("pile of hair")
High-flying, small, fluffy clouds.

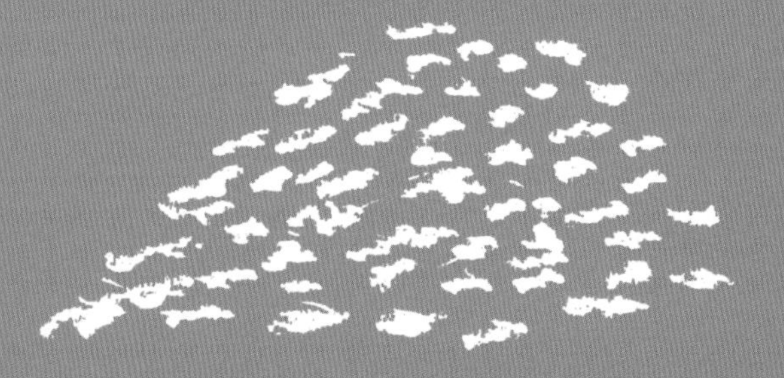

Altocumulus ("high pile")
Thin streaks or patches of cloud.

Stratocumulus ("layered pile")
Layers of thicker, fluffy cloud.

Cumulus ("pile")
Fluffy clouds like piles of cotton wool, often seen on warm days.

Stratus ("layer")
Flat, low, often grayish clouds that blanket the sky and often fall as rain.

OUT OF CURIOSITY

Next time you get a chance to have a good look at the clouds, look for different types and see if you can recognize what they are. (But remember not to look straight at the Sun, because it can damage your eyes.)

WATER FROM THE SKY

What goes up, must come down! The water that rises into the sky as water vapor eventually returns to the ground as rain, snow, sleet, or hail. Scientists call any kind of water from the air or sky "precipitation."

BIG ENOUGH TO FALL

Clouds are made of water droplets, but they are so tiny that they can float in the air. However, in colder air, more and more water condenses onto the droplets, and they get bigger and bigger. Here's what happens:

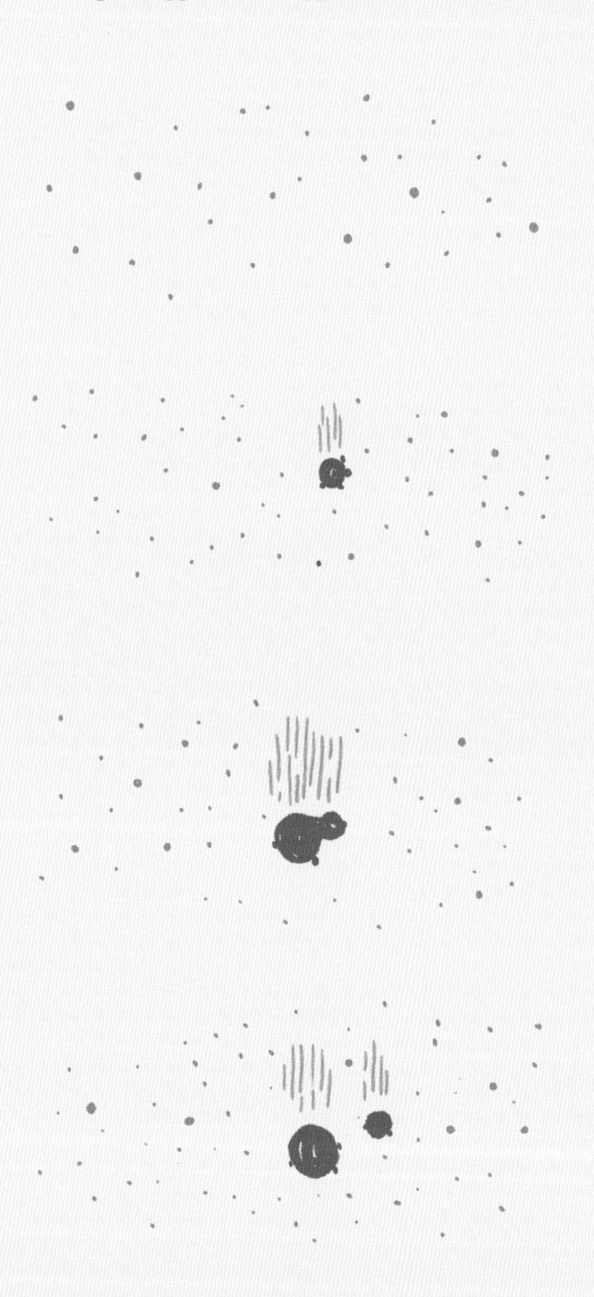

1. CONDENSATION MAKES SOME DROPS START TO GROW BIGGER THAN OTHERS.

2. WHEN A DROP GETS TOO BIG TO STAY IN THE AIR, IT FALLS DOWNWARD.

3. AS IT FALLS, IT HITS OTHER DROPS THAT COMBINE WITH IT. ONCE A DROP REACHES A SIZE OF 0.5 MM (0.02 IN), IT'S OFFICIALLY A RAINDROP!

4. HOWEVER, RAINDROPS CANNOT HOLD TOGETHER IF THEY GET TOO BIG. WHEN THEY REACH AROUND 4–5 MM (0.16–0.2 IN) ACROSS, THEY USUALLY SPLIT APART AGAIN, FORMING ADDITIONAL SMALLER DROPS.

RAINING ON US

If you think about it, it's amazing that clean, fresh water simply falls down out of the sky! Even though we sometimes complain about rain, it's very important.

RAIN FLOWS INTO RIVERS, WHICH SUPPLY WATER FOR DRINKING AND WASHING, AND HABITATS FOR ANIMALS. FLOWING RIVER WATER CAN ALSO GIVE US ELECTRICITY (SEE PAGE 120).

RAIN FRESHENS AND CLEANS THE AIR, WASHING AWAY DUST, POLLEN, AND POLLUTION.

IT WATERS THE GROUND, SO THAT CROPS AND OTHER PLANTS CAN GROW.

BUT SOMETIMES, A RAINY DAY CAN STILL RUIN YOUR PLANS!

OUT OF CURIOSITY

Besides rain and snow, there's also ...

Hail Balls of ice that form in thunderclouds.

Dew Water from the air that condenses onto cold surfaces overnight.

Frost Water from the air that forms ice crystals on freezing surfaces.

Sleet Partly frozen rain.

MAKING SNOWFLAKES

When it's very cold high in the sky, water droplets freeze into ice, and snowflakes form instead of raindrops.

A WATER DROP FREEZES INTO A SIX-SIDED ICE CRYSTAL.

WATER VAPOR FREEZES ONTO THE ICE, FORMING MORE ICE.

THIS HAPPENS FASTEST AT POINTS AND CORNERS, SO THEY GROW OUTWARD, FORMING SPIKY BRANCHES.

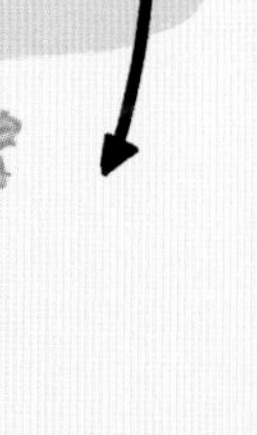

EACH SNOWFLAKE FORMS IN ITS OWN UNIQUE PATTERN.

WIND AND WINDSTORMS

Wind is air in the atmosphere moving around. It can be soft and gentle, like a breeze on a summer day. Or it can be incredibly fast and powerful, strong enough to blow away trees, cars, and even buildings.

HOW WIND WORKS

Wind usually happens because of heat energy from the Sun.

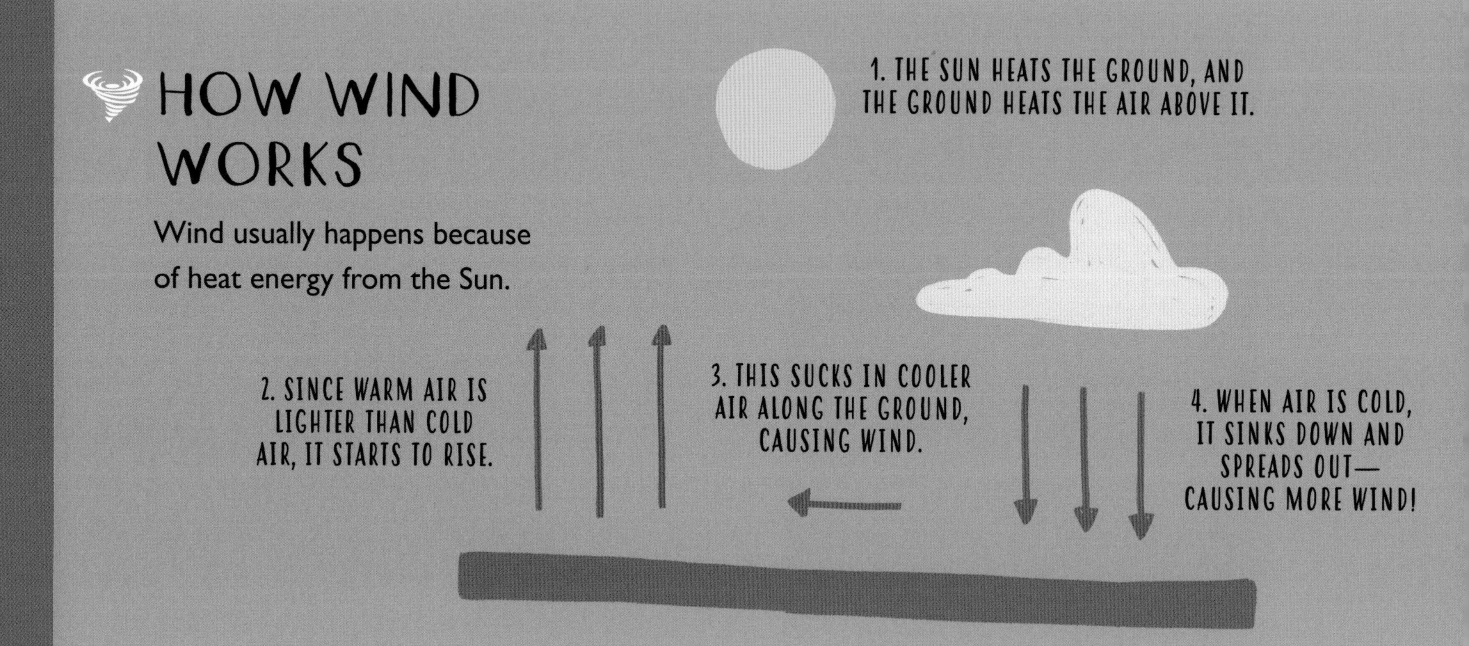

WHIRLING WINDS

A tropical cyclone, also called a hurricane or typhoon, is a giant, rainy windstorm. Cyclones start over warm oceans, as lots of water evaporates and rises into the sky, carried by warm air. This rising air sucks in more damp air from all directions. As it moves inward, it starts to spiral and spin, thanks to the way the Earth spins.

A cyclone becomes a whirling mass of wind and clouds, sometimes up to 1,000 km (620 miles) across.

Cyclones move slowly across the sea. When they reach land, their strong winds and heavy rain can flatten houses and cause floods.

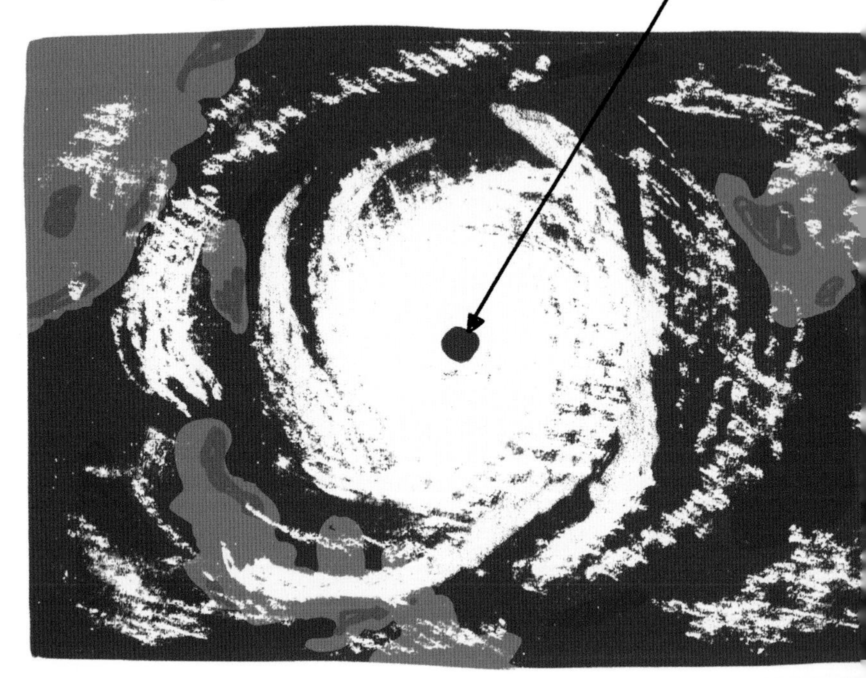

TERRIFYING TORNADOES

The most powerful winds of all are not in cyclones but tornadoes. A tornado is a much smaller, but very dangerous, kind of windstorm. Tornadoes form in thunderstorms, when damp warm air rises up quickly and colder air starts to spiral around it. This creates a spinning funnel of wind, which can be up to 4 km (2.5 mi) across.

Tornadoes can travel across the land or jump from one place to another. Their wind can rip trees from the ground, carry cars into the air, and blow buildings away.

OUT OF CURIOSITY

The fastest wind ever recorded in a hurricane was 408 km/h (254 mph) measured in Australia in 1996.

Tornado winds are harder to measure, but they can reach over 480 km/h (300 mph)!

WEATHER DANGERS

We can control a lot of things about our world, but not the weather. Extreme weather events can sometimes cause natural disasters that destroy homes and claim lives. This weather wheel shows eight of the most dangerous weather disasters.

DUST STORMS

Dust storms and sandstorms happen when the wind blows a large amount of dust or sand through the air. They can cause accidents by making it hard to see and breathe, and when the dust or sand settles, it can bury cars and homes.

WILDFIRES

When trees and plants have dried out thanks to a drought or heatwave, they can easily catch fire. Wildfires spread quickly through hot, dry forests and often burn buildings too. As well as harming humans, they destroy forest habitats and kill a lot of wildlife.

DROUGHTS

A drought is a long period of dry weather, where there's not enough rain to fill rivers and aquifers (see page 34). The ground dries out, crops die, farm animals get thirsty, and sometimes there's not enough water for humans to survive.

HEATWAVES

A heatwave is a period of extra-hot, still weather when the air gets hotter and hotter. It might not sound too bad, but heatwaves are among the deadliest disasters of all. Thousands of people, especially the elderly and sick, can die from overheating.

FLOODS

Heavy rain can saturate the ground, make rivers overflow their banks, and cover large areas of land in water. As well as sweeping people, land, and houses away, floods can destroy crops, kill farm animals, and spread dirt and germs into clean water supplies.

LANDSLIDES

A landslide happens when a large amount of soil, rock, or mud suddenly slips downhill. Rain makes landslides more likely, since it soaks the ground, making it heavier. A landslide can carry homes away or land on top of them and bury them.

LIGHTNING STRIKES

Lightning is a giant, powerful spark of electricity, caused when ice crystals inside thunderclouds build up an electric charge. Being struck directly by lightning can be deadly, and it can also damage buildings, trees, and vehicles.

WINDSTORMS

Hurricanes, typhoons, cyclones, and tornadoes cause disasters every year by blowing off roofs, carrying away cars, and even destroying whole towns.

WEIRD WEATHER

Imagine that you're walking down a busy street, when suddenly, fish start falling from the sky and flopping down all around you! Well, this actually does happen. It can even rain jellyfish and frogs (though not cats and dogs)—and there are many other kinds of weird weather, too.

ANIMAL RAIN

Fish rain, and other types of animal rain, have been reported since ancient times. It's pretty rare, but showers of animals have happened in Singapore, India, California, England, Hungary, Japan, and many other places around the world. But why and how?

SUCKED INTO THE SKY

As you might have noticed, fish, frogs, and jellyfish are all water creatures. Scientists think that sometimes a powerful hurricane or a waterspout (a kind of tornado over water) can pull water into the air from the sea or a lake. If it contains animals such as fish, they then fall back down like rain.

CRAZY CLOUDS

Clouds can form all kinds of interesting shapes, but some are extra-strange. Lenticular clouds, which sometimes form over mountains, are smooth and round and can look a lot like flying saucers.

Mammatus clouds look as if bubbles or bags are dangling down from the sky. And roll clouds, which can form over the coast, look like a giant, long, rolling sausage.

BALL OF FIRE

Normal lighting is either a bright flash in the sky or a jagged spark of electricity jumping between the clouds and the ground. But several people have reported seeing something else during a thunderstorm: a glowing, crackling ball of light that slowly floats though the air and can pass through walls and windows. Sometimes it explodes or disappears with a popping sound.

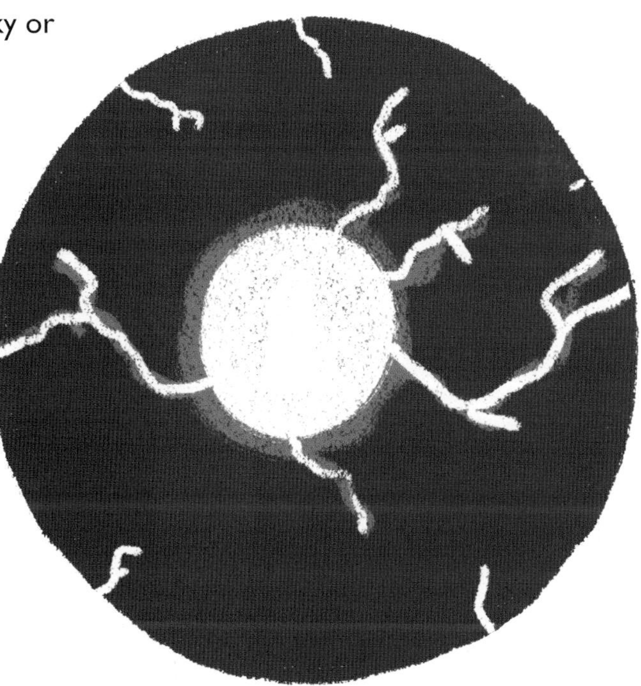

It's known as ball lightning. Scientists still aren't sure how it works, but it seems to be caused by thunderstorms. Now that lots of people have smartphones, more sightings are being caught on camera—so we might be able to make sense of it soon.

WEATHER FORECASTING

Though we can't control the weather, we have found ways to forecast, or predict, what it's going to do. Weather forecasts can help you decide what to wear or whether to have a picnic—or they can save lives by showing where a hurricane or flood will strike.

COLLECTING THE DATA

To make a weather forecast, you need lots of data, or information. Weather scientists called **meteorologists** collect data such as the temperature, wind speed, air pressure, and **humidity,** or amount of water in the air. They use weather stations equipped with measuring devices that collect data on the ground. To collect data in the sky, they use satellites in space and weather balloons that can be launched high into the atmosphere.

A METEOROLOGIST RELEASES A WEATHER BALLOON WITH WEATHER-MEASURING EQUIPMENT ATTACHED TO IT.

COMPUTERS ARE ALSO USED TO TURN WEATHER DATA INTO USEFUL MAPS, SHOWING WHAT'S HAPPENING WHERE.

COMPUTER CALCULATIONS

Next, they feed the data into powerful supercomputers. They use lots of processing power to analyze the data and use it to make predictions. For example, if the data shows wind moving in a particular pattern, the computers can calculate where it will go next and how strong it will be.

AND NOW FOR THE WEATHER!

Finally, all this information is turned into weather forecasts that are broadcast on TV or radio, printed in newspapers, or used in weather apps. Weather forecasts can predict all kinds of things: temperatures, winds, rain and snow, storms, droughts, and heatwaves. They're not always 100 percent right, but they usually give us a good idea of what's ahead.

TV weather forecasters stand next to a map that shows the weather forecast in various different ways, such as arrows for the wind direction and symbols for snow or lightning. This map is showing areas of high and low air pressure, and warm and cold fronts, or masses of moving air.

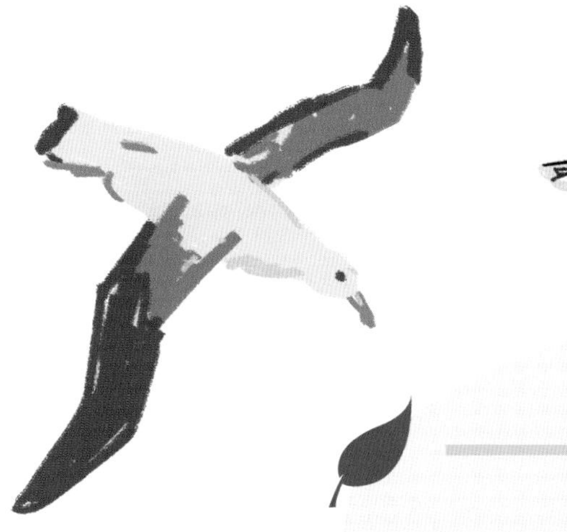

CHAPTER 4

LIFE ON EARTH

As far as we know, Earth is the only planet where living things exist. And they're everywhere! Birds, bats, and insects fly in the air, and enormous whales, giant squid, and countless fish, crabs, and corals fill the seas and oceans. In almost every habitat on Earth, from freezing Antarctica to bone-dry deserts, you'll find living things that have evolved and adapted to survive there. From space, most of the land looks green, thanks to the vast areas of forest and grassland that cover it. Even the soil beneath your feet is bursting with life in the form of earthworms, springtails, mites, and billions of tiny microscopic bacteria. Read on to meet some of these countless life forms!

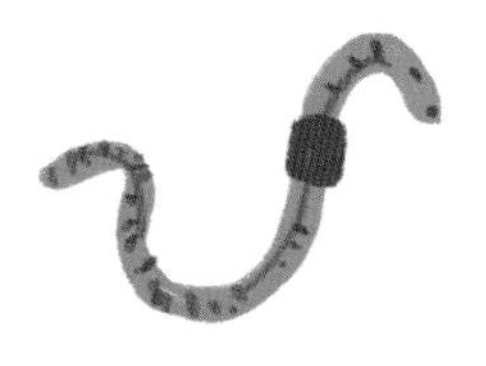

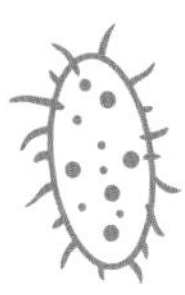 HOW LIFE BEGAN

Scientists think that life began around 3.8 billion years ago. The Earth is about 4.54 billion years old, so that would mean there's been life on Earth for most of its history. However, there weren't always as many different living things as there are now.

HOW DID IT HAPPEN?

To make the first a simple cell, several different natural chemicals must have joined together, along with some kind of energy, such as heat or electricity from lightning.

This might have happened in hot, mineral-filled water from a hydrothermal vent at the bottom of the sea—or maybe in a bubbling hot spring or mud pool.

SMALL AND SIMPLE

The first living things on Earth were very small, single-celled creatures similar to today's **bacteria**. No one knows exactly what they looked like, but they probably had a bubble-like shape, with an outer skin and a variety of chemicals inside.

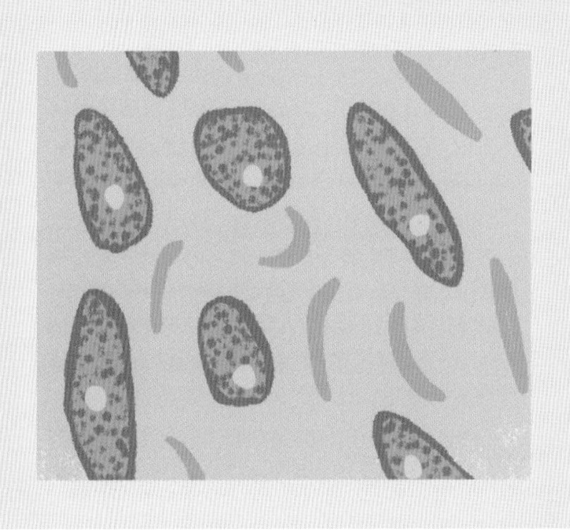

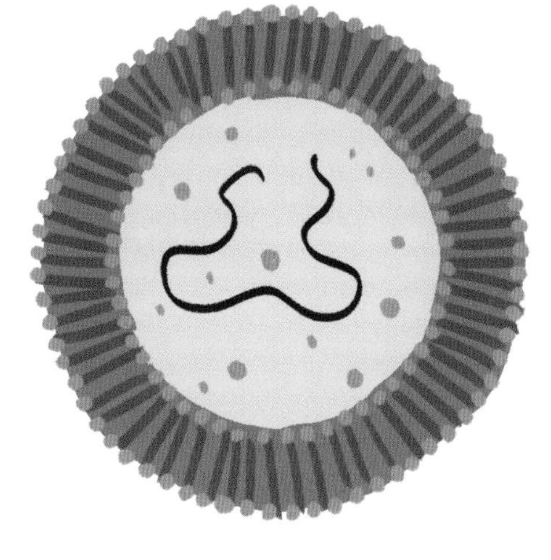

LUCA

This is an artist's impression of a living thing known as LUCA, the Last Universal Common Ancestor. This was a single-celled creature that gradually evolved or developed into different species, which eventually led to all the living things alive today.

EVOLVING AND CHANGING

Living things gradually change over time, and new species, or types of living things, develop. This process is called evolution. Early in the history of life, LUCA evolved into new types of single-celled living things, such as animals, bacteria and **archaea** (left).

LUCA

BACTERIA

ANIMALS

ARCHAEA

MORE AND MORE BRANCHES

Gradually, over billions of years, more and more species evolved, branching off from previous ones. Many-celled creatures appeared, and life spread out to live all over the world.

THE TREE OF LIFE

As evolution happens, new species branch off from old ones. This means that you can see the Earth's life as a kind of tree with lots of branches. It's sometimes called the Tree of Life.

HOW EVOLUTION WORKS

Evolution can happen because of **DNA**, a chemical found inside cells that controls how they live and grow. Whenever living things reproduce, they make copies of themselves. They also copy the DNA in their cells, so that the babies will have the same DNA as the parents.

However, the copying process can sometimes go wrong, making a change in the DNA. Since DNA controls what living things look like and how they work, this can create new types of living things that sometimes become new species.

MILLIONS OF BRANCHES

The Tree of Life includes all the species that have ever existed, including those that are still alive today and those that have died out, such as the dinosaurs. That's millions and millions of species! It would be impossible to draw a tree showing them all. Instead, this tree picture shows the main groups of living things, and some examples of them. Can you find the human?

FAMILIES AND RELATIVES

As you can see, like a real tree, the Tree of Life has several bigger branches, that branch off into many smaller branches and twigs. The living things on the same branch are more closely related than living things on faraway branches.

For example, humans are mammals. We share a small branch with other mammals, such as gorillas and horses, and a bigger branch with other vertebrates, like birds and fish. But things like trees and jellyfish are on completely different branches, since we are less similar to them.

Take a look at the tree, and see if you can find some other closely related groups.

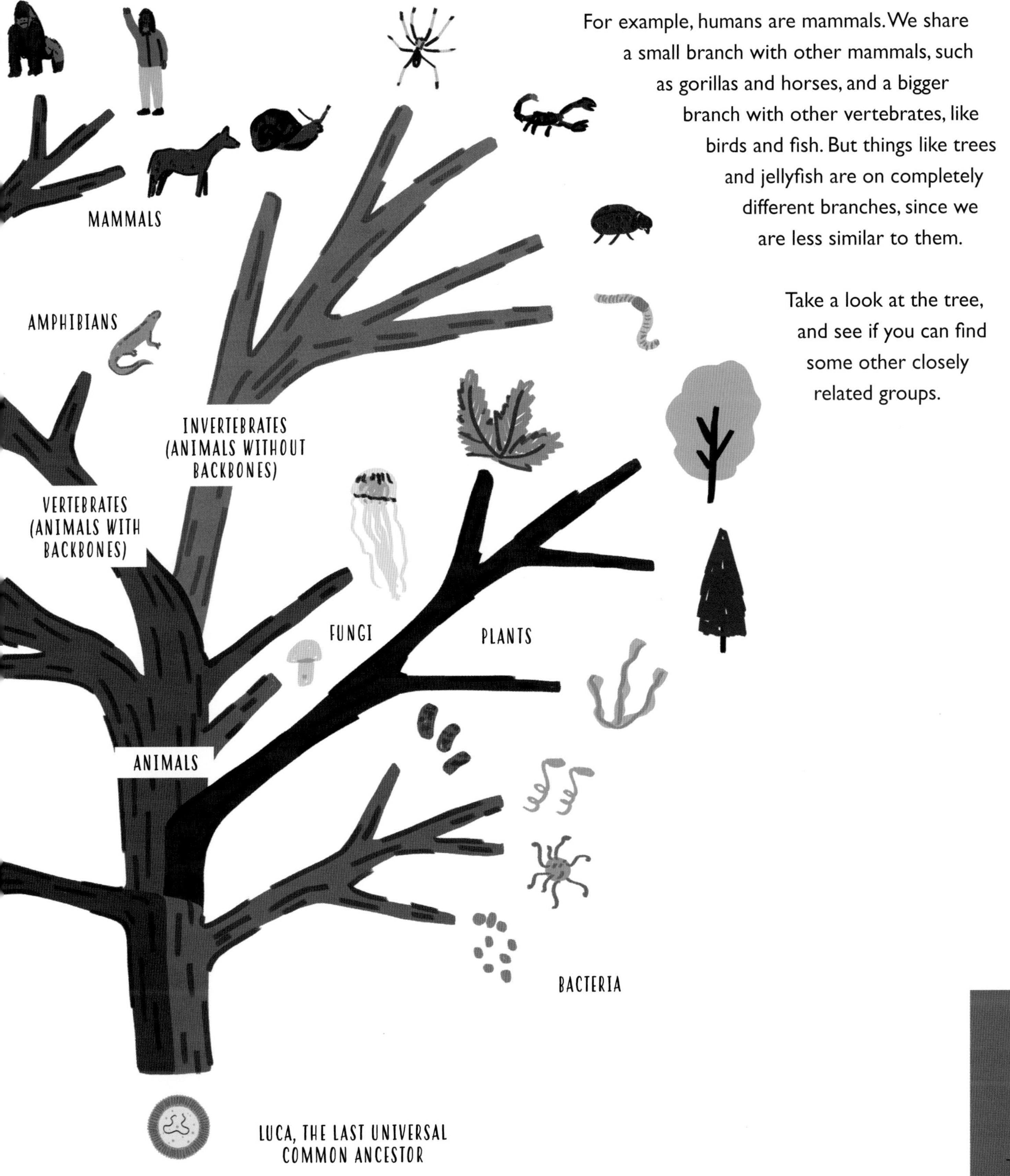

MICROORGANISMS

Microorganisms are the smallest types of living things. In fact, their name means living things that can only be seen through a microscope. Though we can't see them, we are surrounded by billions and billions of them. They live in soil and water, in our homes, and in and on other living things.

MEET THE MICROORGANISMS!

There are thousands of different species of microorganisms and many more we haven't even discovered yet. You can see some of the main types here.

BACTERIA ARE VERY SMALL, SIMPLE, SINGLE-CELLED LIVING THINGS.

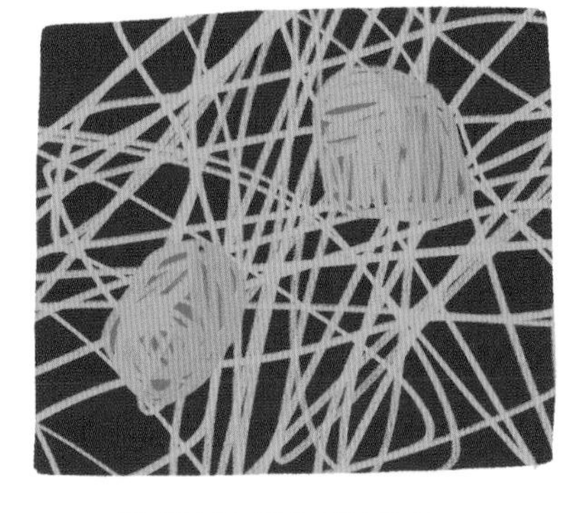

ARCHAEA ARE SIMILAR TO BACTERIA.

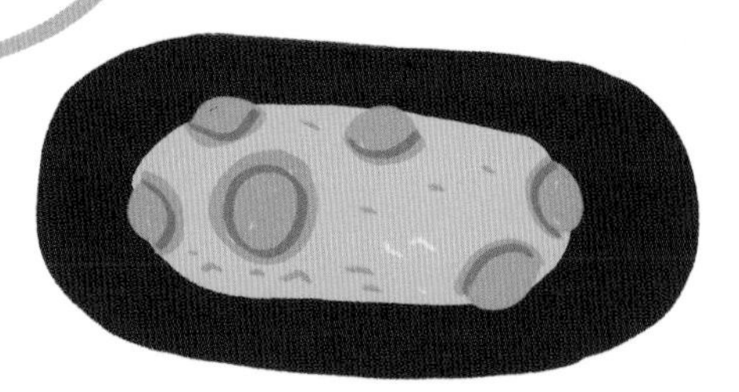

YEASTS ARE SINGLE-CELLED FUNGI, AND ARE RELATED TO MUSHROOMS AND MOLDS.

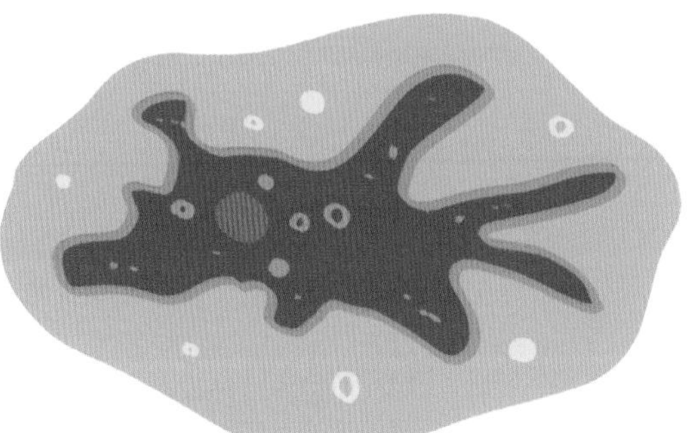

AMOEBAS ARE LARGER SINGLE-CELLED CREATURES THAT CAN MOVE AROUND AND SWALLOW FOOD.

DIATOMS ARE SINGLE-CELLED ALGAE THAT MAKE FOOD USING SUNLIGHT, LIKE PLANTS DO.

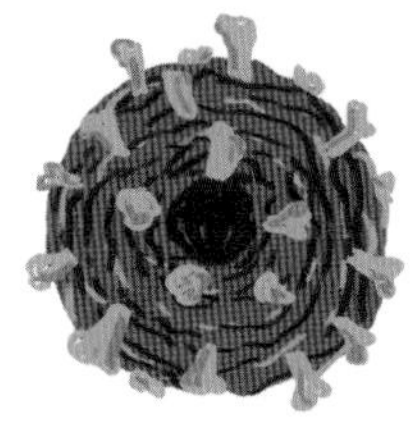

VIRUSES, LIKE THIS CORONAVIRUS, ARE THE SMALLEST MICROORGANISMS. THEY SURVIVE BY INVADING LIVING CELLS.

EXTREMOPHILES

Some bacteria and archaea are **extremophiles**, meaning "lovers of extremes." They are good at surviving at very high or low temperatures, or in very salty or dry places.

Grand Prismatic Spring in Wyoming, USA, has several types of extremophile bacteria and archaea living in it, which give it its bright rainbow shades.

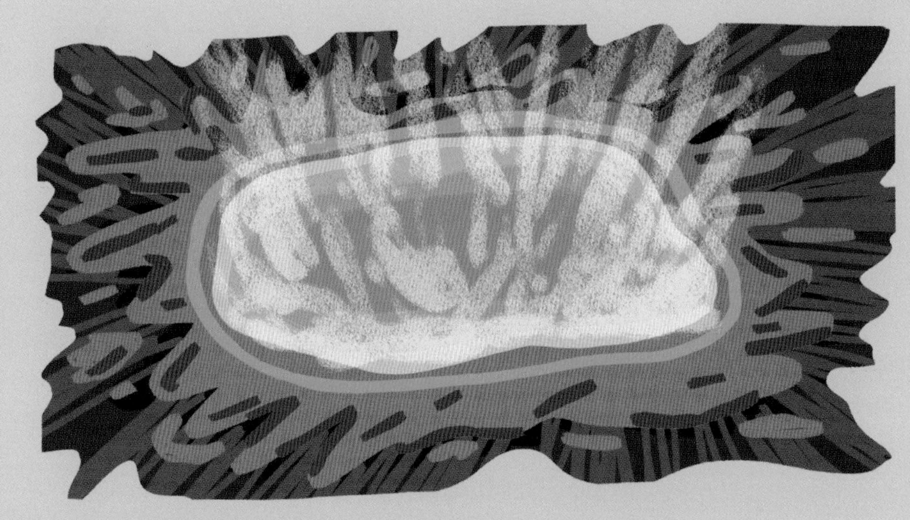

CHICKENPOX IS CAUSED BY A TYPE OF VIRUS.

GERMS AND DISEASES

Some microorganisms, especially some bacteria and viruses, can invade our bodies and give us diseases, from colds and sore throats to more serious illnesses like the flu and cholera.

USEFUL MICROORGANISMS

Many microorganisms are useful, to the planet and to us.

• Bacteria and fungi help dead plants and animals decay and break down into the soil, helping new plants to grow.

• Some helpful bacteria live in our intestines, helping us digest food.

• We also use many types of microorganisms to do useful jobs. One example is bread yeast. When we add it to bread dough, it makes bubbles of gas. They make the dough rise, so the bread is soft and springy.

PLANTS AND FUNGI

Plants and fungi are two different groups of living things, but they can seem similar. Unlike animals, both plants and fungi mainly stay in one place and find their food without moving around.

WHAT ARE PLANTS?

Plants are living things that make their own food chemicals using energy from sunlight, a process called **photosynthesis**. They do this in their leaves, using a green chemical called **chlorophyll**. That's why plants are green!

There are several types of plants including flowering plants, conifers, mosses, and ferns.

THANK YOU, PLANTS!

Plants are vital to other life on Earth. They provide food for many other living things. They also take in carbon dioxide gas from the air and give out oxygen, which animals and humans need to breathe.

FLOWERING PLANTS INCLUDE SMALL FLOWERS LIKE POPPIES AND DAISIES, AND FLOWERING TREES LIKE APPLE AND CHERRY TREES.

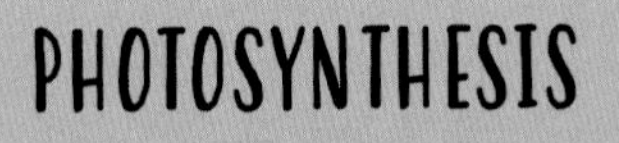

Photosynthesis is a process that plants use to make food from sunlight. Here's how it works.

THE LEAF TAKES IN CARBON DIOXIDE FROM THE AIR, AND WATER FROM THE SOIL, THROUGH THE PLANT'S ROOTS AND STEMS.

USING ENERGY FROM SUNLIGHT, THE PLANT CHANGES THESE INTO CHEMICALS IT CAN USE AS FOOD, SO IT CAN GROW AND MAKE NEW PLANT PARTS.

THIS MAKES THE GAS OXYGEN, WHICH IS RELEASED INTO THE AIR.

TREES ARE GIANT PLANTS! THE TALLEST SPECIES, THE COAST REDWOOD, CAN GROW TO THE HEIGHT OF 115 M (380 FT).

WHAT ARE FUNGI?

People sometimes think that fungi, such as mushrooms and toadstools, are a type of plant. But, they are actually a very different group of living things. Unlike plants, fungi don't use sunlight to make food. Instead, they take in food from their surroundings, like animals do.

Toadstools, below, have a network of hairlike roots called **hyphae**. They grow down into the rotting log to feed on it.

GRASS IS A TYPE OF FLOWERING PLANT. ITS SMALL, GREEN FLOWERS APPEAR IF YOU LET IT GROW LONG.

ANIMALS

Think of an animal, and what do you imagine? A dog, a cat, an elephant, a horse, a creepy-crawly spider, or a huge shark? Most people know an animal when they see one, but what makes something an animal?

WHAT ANIMALS DO

An animal is different from other living things in three main ways. If it does all of these, it's probably an animal!

• Animals move around, often quite fast, by walking, running, swimming, jumping, flying, or slithering.

• They eat! Most animals live by taking in food from their surroundings, and they usually have a mouth.

• Animals have good senses, such as sight, smell, and hearing, and can react quickly.

OUT OF CURIOSITY

Some animals, called herbivores, eat plants, while others, called carnivores, hunt and eat other animals. This hungry tiger is about to pounce on a plant-eating deer.

Animals may also be omnivores, meaning they eat both meat and plants.

 TYPES OF ANIMALS

Scientists divide animals into two main groups: **vertebrates** and **invertebrates**. Vertebrates have a backbone and usually a whole skeleton attached to it. Invertebrates don't have a backbone. They can have a hard shell, a tough outer skin, or a soft, squashy body, like a worm.

Check out these examples of animals from the two groups:

VERTEBRATES

Vertebrates include five types of animals: mammals, birds, reptiles, amphibians, and fish.

Mammals, like the elephant, are usually hairy or furry. Mother mammals feed their babies on milk from their bodies.

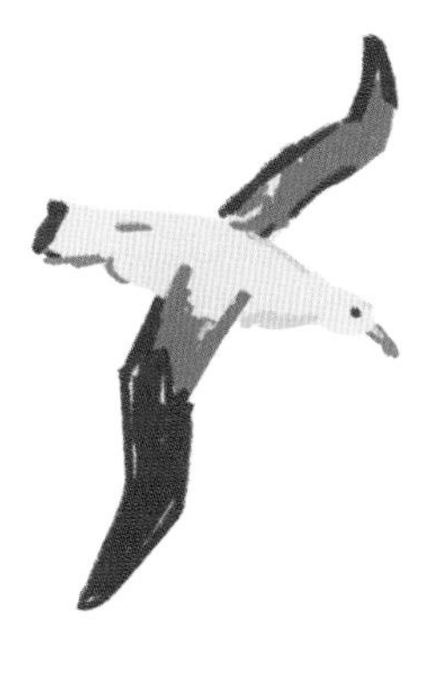

Birds have feathers and lay eggs. Albatrosses are amazing at flying, but some birds, like ostriches, are flightless.

Chameleons are lizards, a type of reptile. **Reptiles** usually have dry, scaly skin. The dinosaurs were reptiles, too!

Amphibians, such as frogs and toads, spend part of their lives in water, and have smooth, slimy skin.

Fish mainly live in water. They breathe underwater using their gills, and swim using their fins. Sharks are a type of fish.

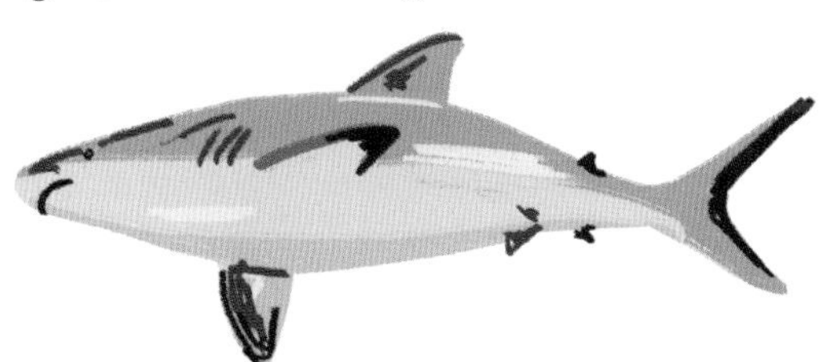

INVERTEBRATES

Spiders, centipedes, and insects like this bee are all invertebrates. They have a tough outer skin called an exoskeleton.

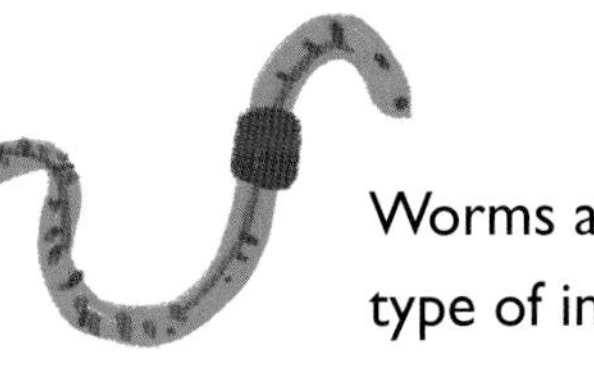

Worms are another type of invertebrate.

The large **mollusk** family of invertebrates includes slugs, snails, shellfish such as clams, octopuses, and squid. Most invertebrates are very small, but if they live in the sea, they can grow bigger because the water supports their bodies.

BIOMES

Biomes are large, natural areas of the world that have different kinds of wildlife living in them. They are similar to climate zones (see page 52), but as well as climate, each biome has its own landscapes and vegetation (the type of plants that live there), and particular types of animals and other living things.

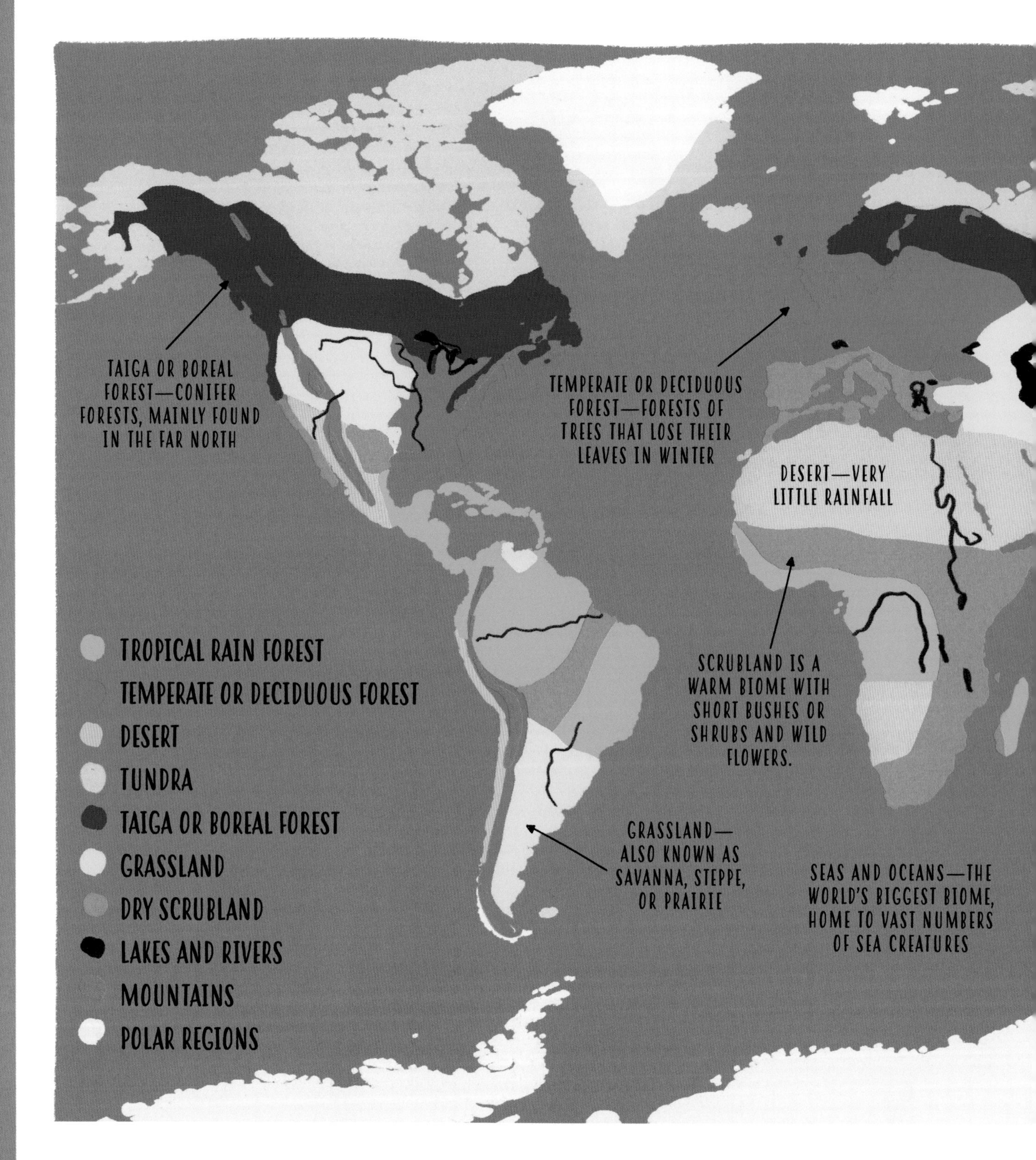

BIOMES ON THE MAP

There are various ways of dividing the world up into **biomes**. This world map shows where nine different biomes can be found. Within each one, there are smaller variations, such as mountains and rivers.

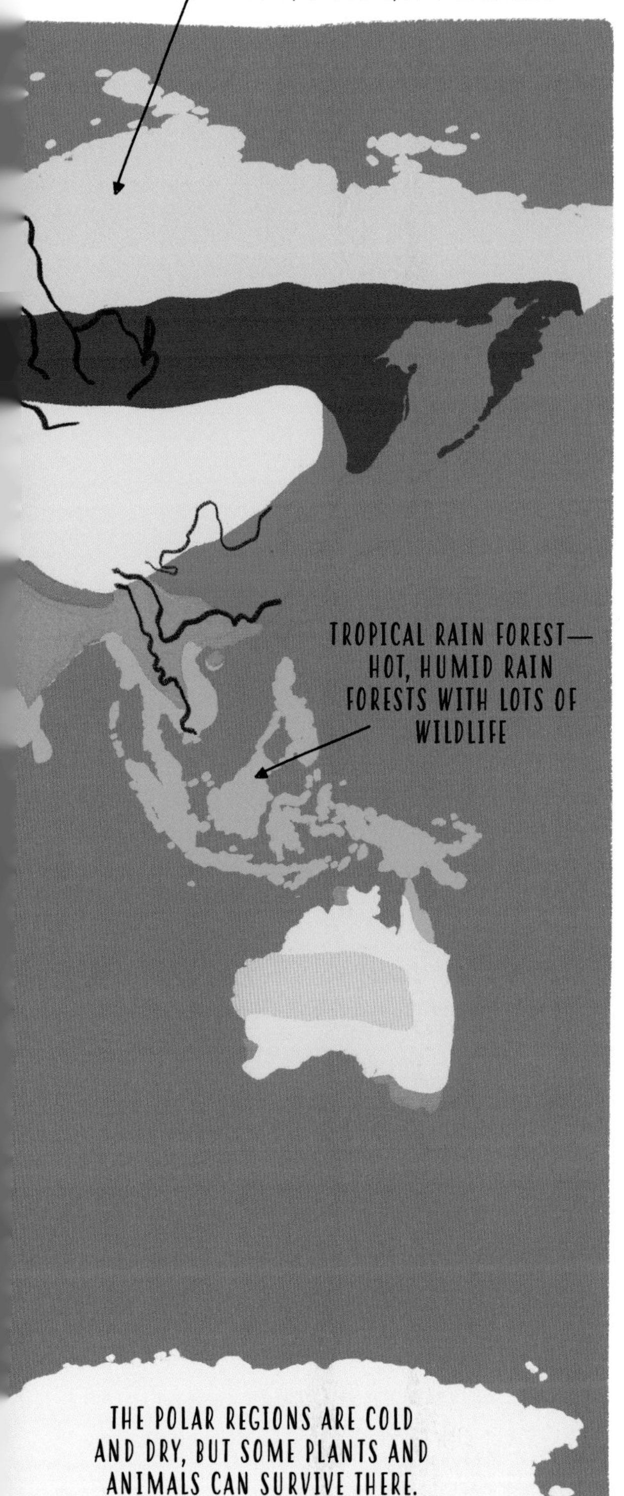

ADAPTATION

Through evolution, living things have adapted and changed to be well-suited to their biome, with features that help them survive there.

For example, it's hard for plants to live in hot, dry deserts, but cactuses can. They have evolved a waxy coating that keeps them from drying out, leaves that store water, and spines that keep animals away.

Meanwhile, Adelie penguins are perfectly adapted to life in icy Antarctica. A thick layer of blubber under their skin and oily, waterproof feathers keep them warm. Instead of flying, they use their wings like flippers to swim and steer underwater.

HABITATS

Each living species has a natural home or surroundings that it has evolved to live in, where it finds it easiest to survive. This natural home is called its habitat.

LARGE HABITATS

Depending on the species, habitats can be big or small. For example, humpback whales live in the sea and travel long distances between their feeding and mating areas. They can survive in warm water close to the equator, and colder water around the poles. The whole ocean is their habitat.

Humpback whales are BIG: up to 16 m (52 ft) long. They need a big habitat with plenty of space to roam around, hunt, and meet a mate. This humpback is breaching, or leaping out of the water and splashing back down. This is why a humpback whale can't live in an aquarium—it needs much more room!

SMALL HABITATS

Some habitats are much smaller. A frog's habitat might be a small pond. For a velvet worm, it could be a cave. An old stone wall could be a habitat for mosses and lichens. Sometimes, a living thing is a habitat for other living things, such as a tree where bark beetles, ants, and squirrels live.

I NEED MY HABITAT!

Some creatures are good at living in lots of different habitats. Rats, for example, can survive on many different kinds of food, and are happy in many habitats: forests, meadows, caves, in houses, or on ships.

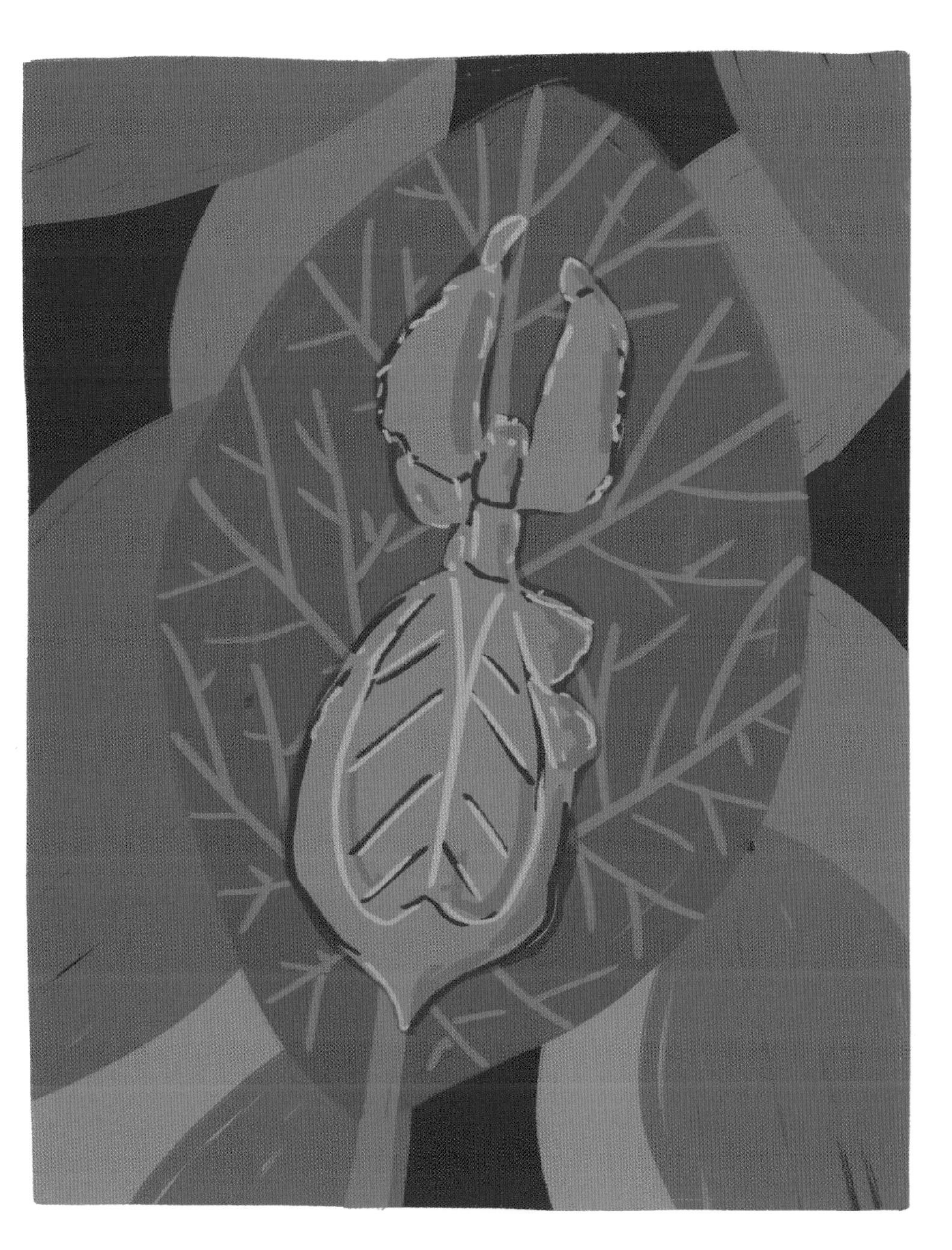

But other animals need the particular habitat they have evolved to live in. Giant pandas are like this. They eat mainly bamboo, and they need a Chinese bamboo forest habitat. That's why some species can become endangered (see page 116) if their habitats are badly damaged or destroyed.

Leaf insects live in forests in Asia and Australia. They are camouflaged as leaves to hide from hungry predators. They have evolved to match their forest home—so if the forest is cut down, it's hard for them to survive.

ECOSYSTEMS

An ecosystem means a habitat and the living things that live in it. They work together as a whole system, with each species depending on the habitat, and on other other species, to survive.

FOOD CHAINS

In an **ecosystem**, species feed on each other in sequences called food chains. For example, in the Antarctic Ocean, orcas eat seals, which eat fish, which eat krill (small shrimplike animals), which feed on plankton (tiny plants and animals floating in seawater). Animal plankton feed on plant plankton, which use sunlight to grow.

?

OUT OF CURIOSITY

One way of thinking about the Earth is to see it as a single, giant ecosystem. We all share the same planet, air, water, and food, and we depend on other species to survive.

FOOD WEBS

A food web is a network of interlinking food chains. In this picture, you can see part of the food web in an African savanna, or grassland.

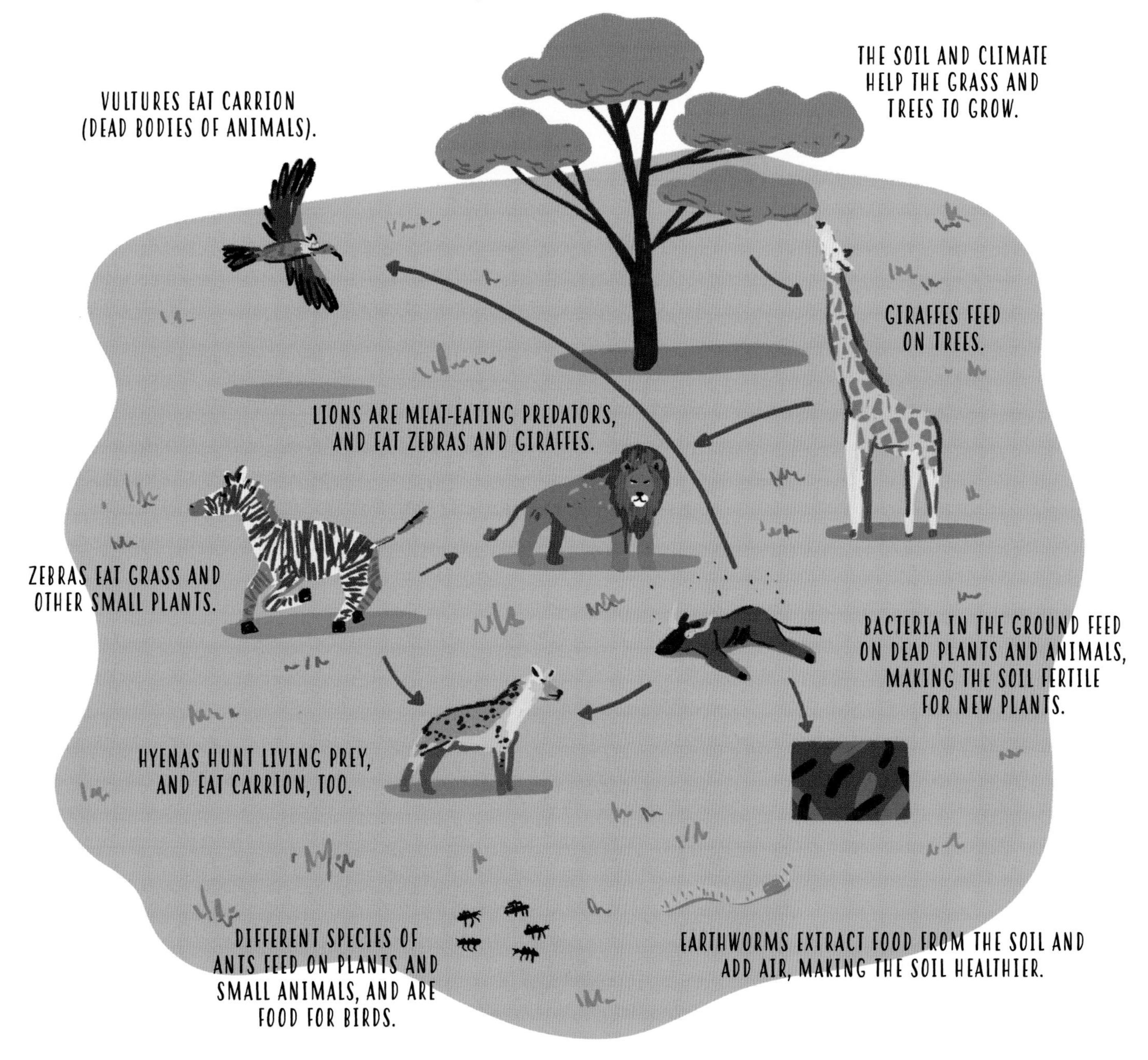

BALANCING ACT

As you can see, an ecosystem exists in a balance. If one species is removed, it affects the others. If there were no lions in the grassland food web, there would be more zebras and not enough grass to feed them. If there were no trees, giraffes wouldn't have enough food, and vultures wouldn't have places to build their nests.

This is one reason why **biodiversity**—a wide range of different species—is important. Each species plays an important part in its ecosystem, so that they can all keep existing.

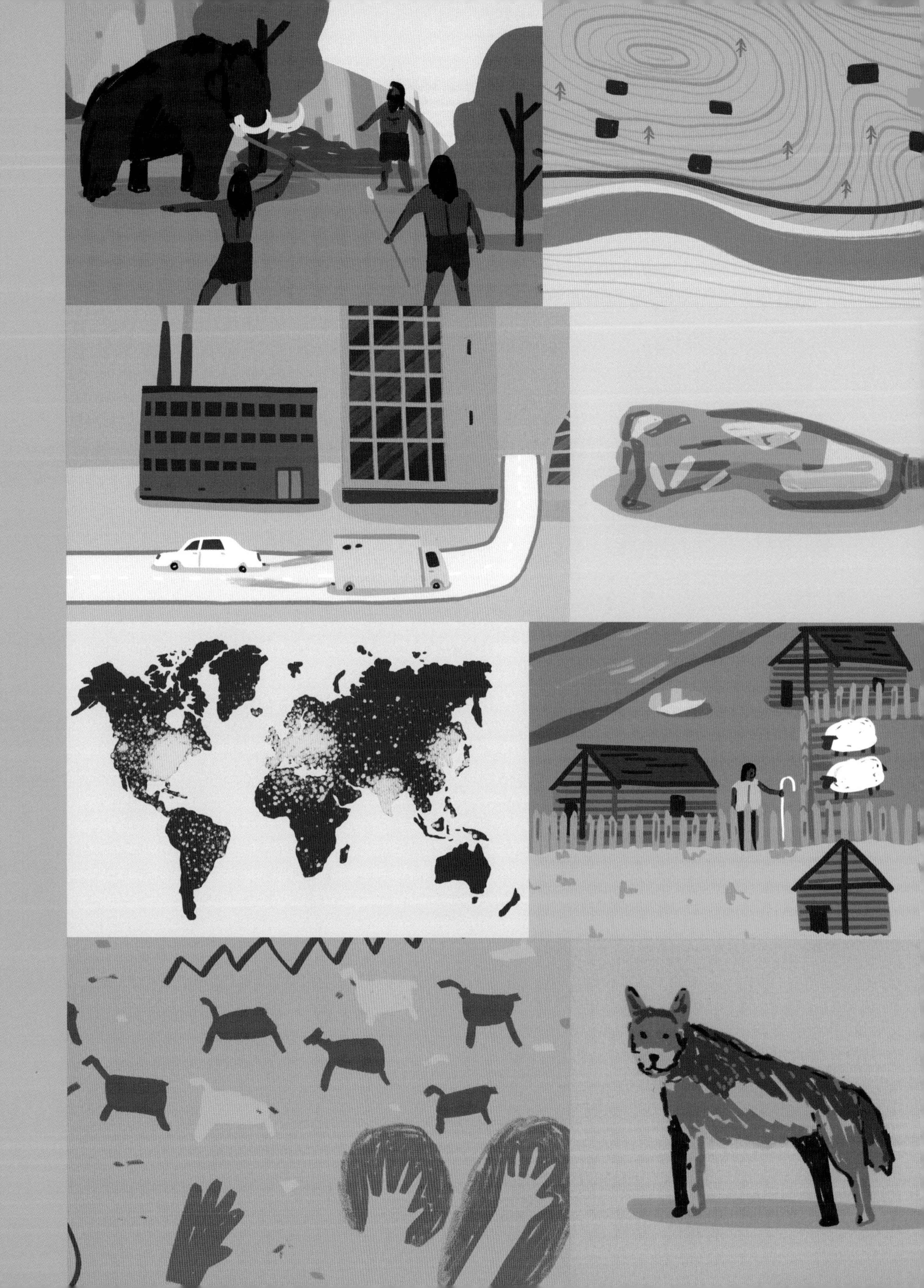

CHAPTER 5

HUMANS ON EARTH

Humans are animals. We belong to the ape family, and we're closely related to chimpanzees, gorillas, and orangutans. We're just one of the millions of different living species that have evolved on Planet Earth.

But there is something a little bit different about us! Instead of evolving sharp claws or super-powerful senses for finding food, humans evolved big brains and nimble hands. We began using fire to cook, building houses, farming plants and animals, and inventing all kinds of tools, machines, and gadgets. Of course, this has led to many amazing and useful things, but it also means that we've changed our planet in ways that no other species has.

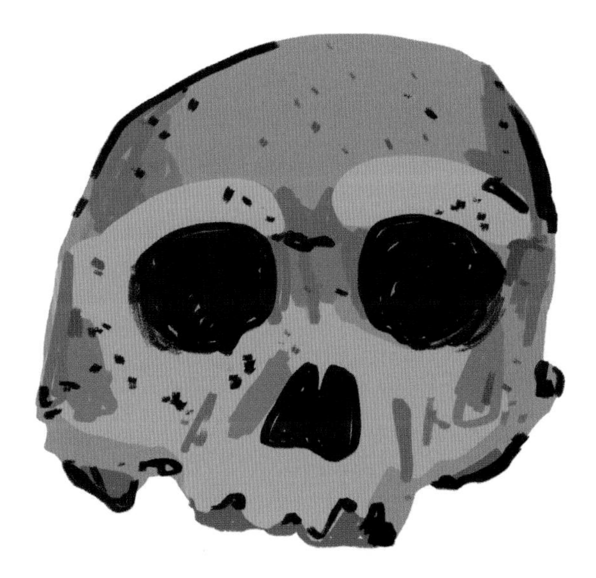

HOW HUMANS EVOLVED

Like other species, humans gradually evolved over time from earlier forms of life. The first humans evolved about 2–3 million years ago. That might seem like a long time to us, but compared to the history of the Earth, it's very recent.

THE HUMAN FAMILY TREE

The first humans didn't look just like us. In fact, they were a different species! There have been several different species of humans, who all lived for different amounts of time as humans evolved. Most of them died out, and today only one species is left: modern humans. The scientific name for our species, *Homo sapiens*, means "smart human."

No one knows exactly how modern humans evolved—we can only make guesses based on old fossils. This family tree shows some of the different species of early humans and how they could have been related.

Australopithecus africanus ("Southern ape")
Around 3.5–2 million years ago
Australopithecus were apes that probably evolved into the first humans.

Homo habilis
("Handy human")
Around 2.4–1.4 million years ago. One of the earliest known humans.

Homo ergaster
("Working human")
Around 2–1.3 million years ago.

Homo heidelbergensis
("Heidelberg human")
Around 700,000–-200,000 years ago.

Homo erectus
("Upright human")
Around 1.9 million–100,000 years ago.

Homo neanderthalensis, or **Neanderthals**
("Neander Valley human")
Around 400,000–40,000 years ago. Our closest-known human relatives, and the most recent to die out.

Homo sapiens ("Smart human")
Around 300,000 years ago to the present.

TOOLMAKERS

As humans evolved, we got better and better at inventing, making, and using tools. Some animals use tools, too—for example, chimps use sticks to fish termites out of their nests to eat. But early humans became extremely good at it, developing from making simple stone hammers and axes to carefully shaped arrowheads, knives, and needles.

PEAR-SHAPED HAND AXES HAVE BEEN FOUND THROUGHOUT AFRICA AND EURASIA.

ARROWHEADS

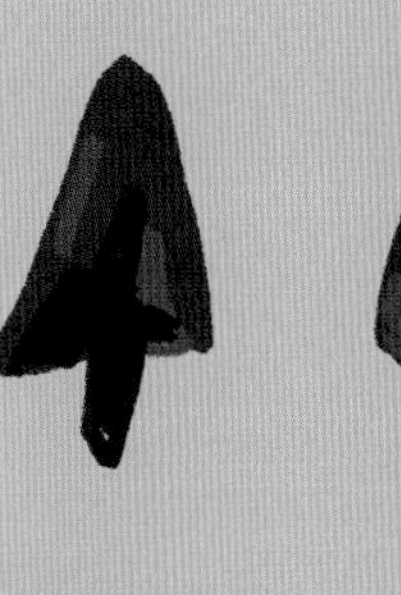

KNIFE BLADES

ART AND CULTURE

At the same time, humans developed culture, such as making art, music, and decoration, and burying dead people in graves. We also developed complex languages, allowing us to share and pass on ideas.

Ancient cave art at the Cueva de las Manos ("Cave of the hands") in Argentina shows herds of guanacos (a type of llama), patterns, and symbols, and shapes made by blowing a spray of paint around a hand.

SPREADING OUT

Fossils show that humans first evolved in eastern Africa. From there, waves of different human species slowly spread out to different parts of the world. *Homo sapiens*, or modern humans, evolved and spread out the most recently.

The arrows on this world map show some of the the main routes humans took as they spread throughout the world.

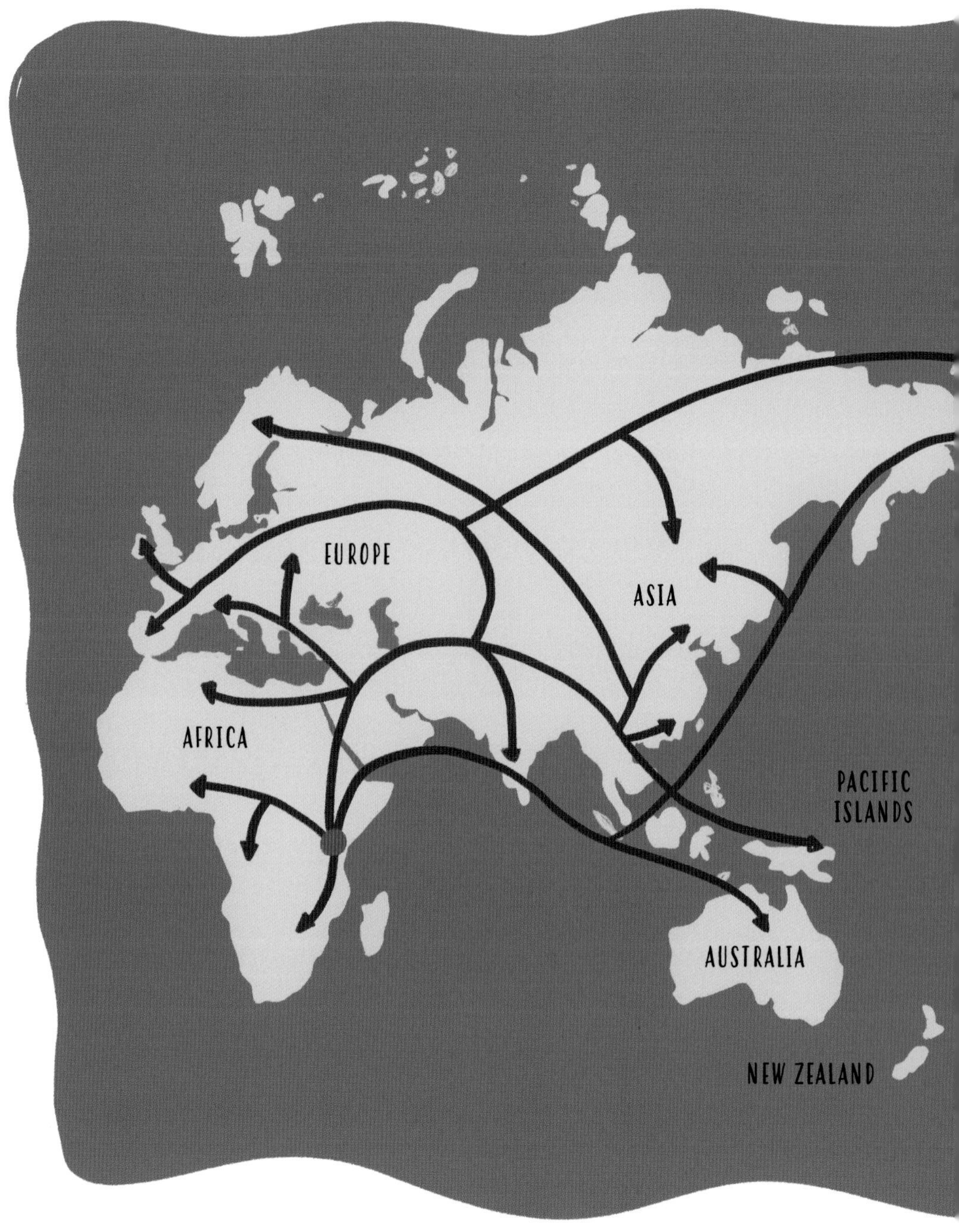

In prehistoric times, people didn't have planes, cars, or even tame horses, so these journeys did not happen quickly. People moved on foot, in small groups in search of food or water—or maybe to avoid dangers such as floods or other humans. Spreading across a continent would have taken many generations.

Some people found their way on early boats or rafts, reaching Australia by about 65,000 years ago.

During the last Ice Age (an extra-cold period in Earth's history), around 20,000 to 15,000 years ago, more of the world's water was frozen into ice, and the sea level was lower. Asia and North America were connected in the far north by dry land, allowing people to walk across into the Americas.

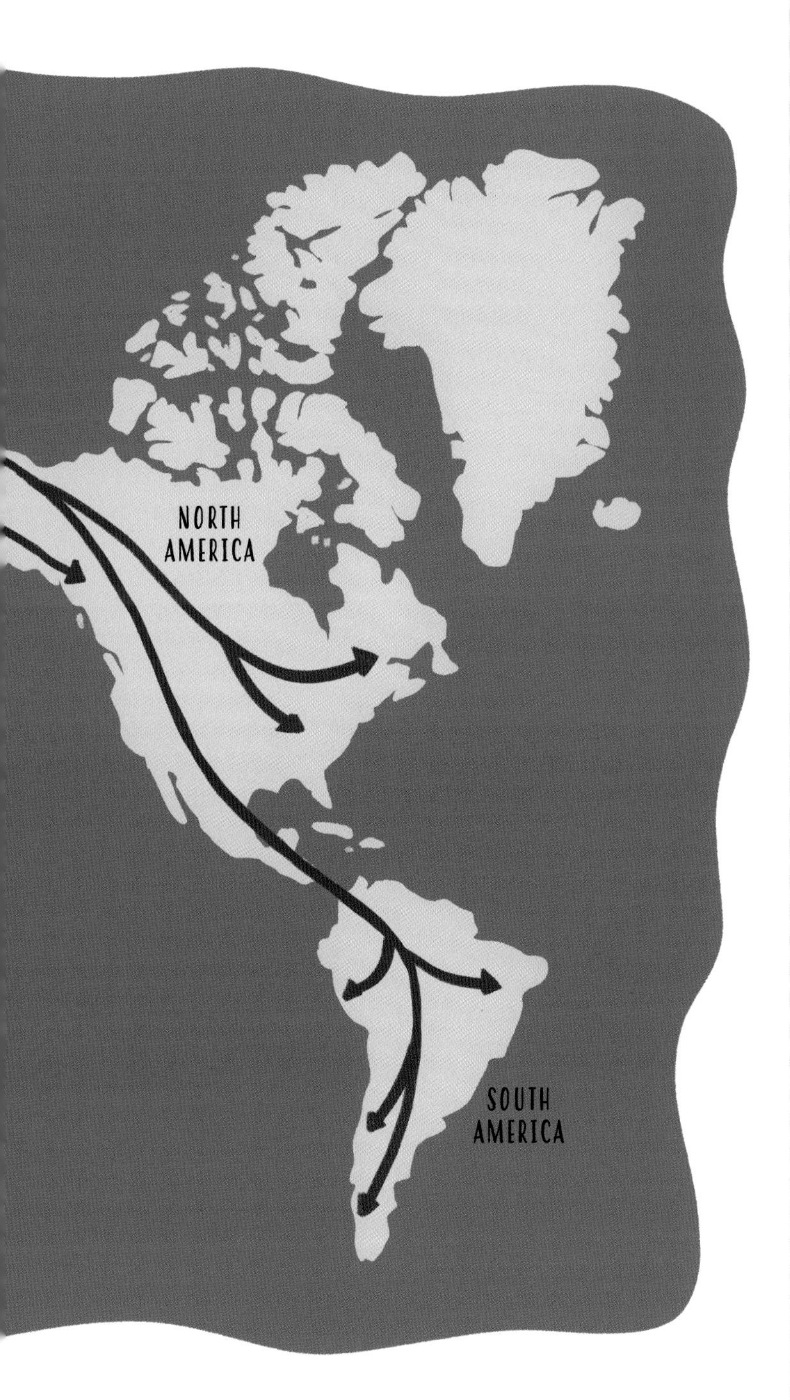

However, some parts of the world remained uninhabited until much more recently. For example, humans did not live in New Zealand until around the year 1250, less than 1,000 years ago.

HOW DO WE KNOW?

We can tell where humans were, and when, by studying **fossil** skulls and skeletons. Some early humans left other evidence behind, too, such as stone tools and cave paintings.

Human fossils are quite rare, and often only a small part of the skeleton is found. It can take a lot of detective work to figure out where each fossil fits into the story. But we are still finding new fossils that reveal more and more about our past.

This 146,000-year-old human skull was found in China in the 1930s, hidden, then rediscovered and studied in 2018. It's known as the "Dragon Man" skull, and some experts think it could belong to a previously unknown human species.

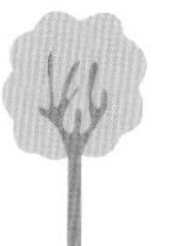

USING RESOURCES

What are resources? This word simply means useful stuff, materials, or supplies. For example, if you were living in Europe 30,000 years ago, firewood would be an important resource. You'd burn it to keep warm, to cook food, and to scare away wild animals.

RESOURCES AND THEIR USES

Here are some of the natural resources humans have been using since ancient times. We still use many of them now. Look at the examples, and see if you can think of other uses for each resource, and how we use it today.

Wood from trees
- Used as firewood or to make furniture

Stone from the ground
- Used to build homes, forts, and animal enclosures

Fish caught in seas, rivers, or lakes
- Used as food, or for oil in lamps

Animal skins from wolves, seals, rabbits, and other furry creatures
- Used to make warm clothes and beds

RESOURCES FROM THE EARTH

Humans have always used natural resources from the world around us. We've used them for food, fuel, and to make weapons, clothes, tools, homes, and everyday items. In prehistoric times, there weren't that many people, and they were spread out over a wide area, so what they used didn't affect the planet very much.

Clay, a kind of smooth, heavy, muddy soil from the ground
- Used to make pottery

OUT OF CURIOSITY

Over time, the human population has grown and grown, especially in the last few hundred years. And the more people there are, the more stuff we use. We've now used up so much of some resources, they're in danger of running out.

Gold found in the ground or in rivers
- Used to make beautiful, precious rings and necklaces

Ocher, a type of reddish or yellowish clay
- Used for making cave art and body paint

Bone from animals such as swans and elephants
- Used to make needles, pins, and flutes

FARMING

About 12,000 years ago, a huge change began to happen around the world. Instead of hunting animals and collecting wild plants for food, people started farming.

BEFORE FARMING

For most of human history, people had been hunter-gatherers. They ate food they could catch or find in the wild: fish from rivers, shellfish from beaches, honey from bees' nests, and wild fruits, berries, and nuts.

WHY THEN?

Farming happened at different times in different parts of the world—probably earlier than 12,000 years ago in some places, and much later in others. However, around 12,000 years ago, the world was warming up after the last Ice Age. Areas that had been covered in ice became warmer and wetter, making it easier to grow crops.

OUT OF CURIOSITY

The time from the start of farming to the present day has its own name: the Holocene epoch. Holocene means "totally new". It's called that because this is the time period in which the world has changed most, thanks to the activities of humans.

AFTER FARMING

When people began farming, it changed their whole way of life.

SINCE THEY WEREN'T ALWAYS HUNTING AND GATHERING FOOD, PEOPLE HAD MORE FREE TIME, TOO. THEY COULD SPEND MORE TIME DISCOVERING AND INVENTING THINGS, MAKING ART AND MUSIC, STUDYING THE STARS, AND OTHER ACTIVITIES.

TO GROW CROPS, YOU HAD TO STAY IN ONE PLACE FOR A LONG TIME. SO PEOPLE BEGAN SETTLING DOWN AND BUILDING VILLAGES, WITH STRONGER, MORE PERMANENT HOUSES.

SINCE IT WAS EASIER TO GET ENOUGH FOOD, IT WAS EASIER TO SURVIVE. THE POPULATION GREW, AND VILLAGES GOT BIGGER.

INSTEAD OF SPENDING HOURS CHASING WILD ANIMALS, THEY WERE ALWAYS AVAILABLE. BESIDES MEAT, FARM ANIMALS COULD PROVIDE A STEADY SUPPLY OF EGGS, MILK, WOOL, FEATHERS, AND USEFUL SKINS.

TOWNS AND CITIES

As more and more people settled into the farming lifestyle, villages became towns, and towns became the first cities. From around 4000 BCE, or 6,000 years ago, early cities developed in many parts of the world, including present-day China, Egypt, Mali, Pakistan, Greece, Syria, and Iraq.

THE CITY OF UR

Ur was a powerful city in what is now southern Iraq, part of the ancient Sumerian civilization. At its height, around 2000 BCE, it could have been home to over 60,000 people. That's not big compared to some cities now, but back then it was one of the largest cities on Earth.

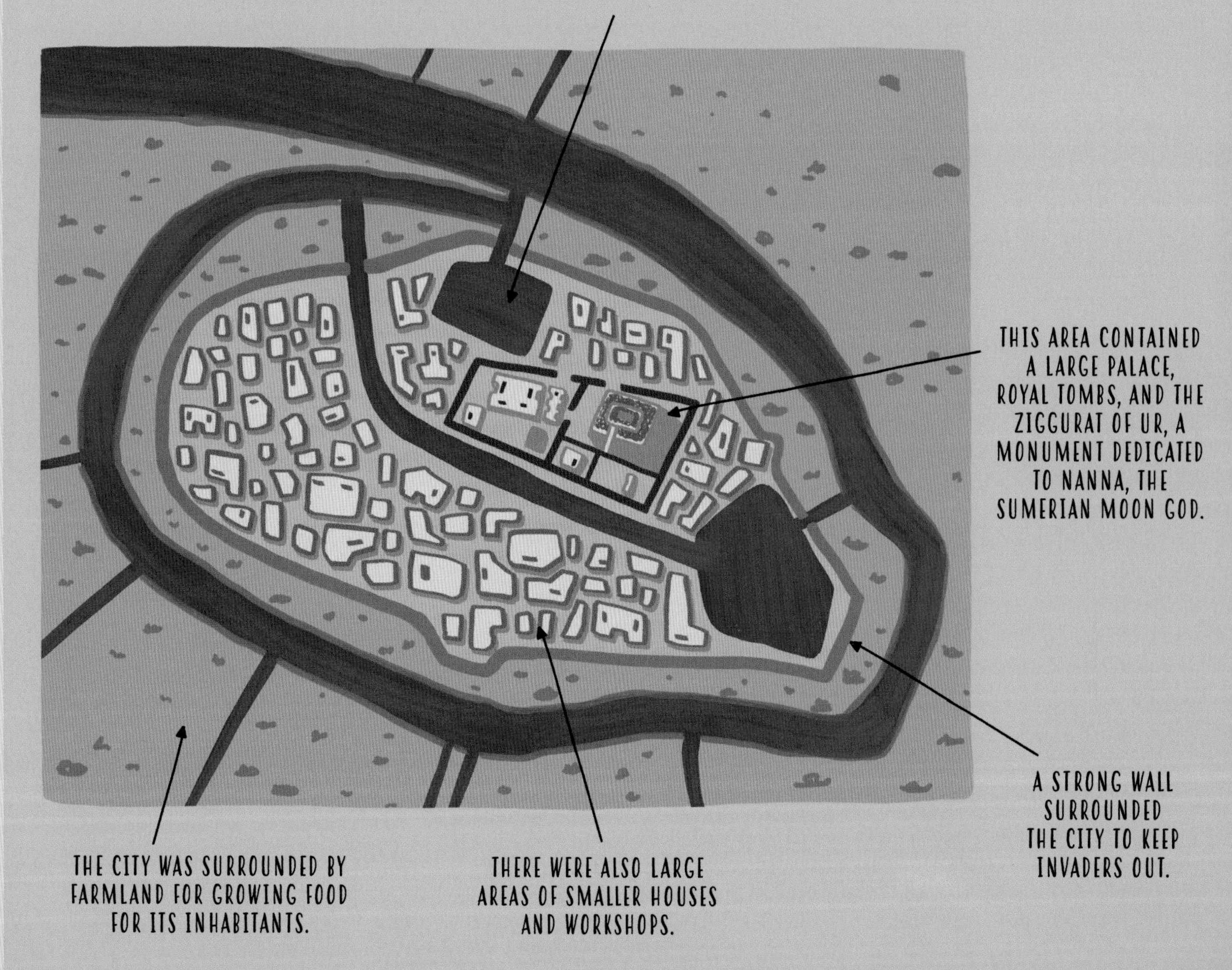

TAKING OVER

Towns, cities, and farms take up lots of space. Humans made this space by clearing forests and other wild habitats. This is one of the biggest changes humans have made to the planet. Since farming first began, around a third of the world's forests have been cut down. We've also taken over many other wild areas, such as grasslands, swamps, coasts, and deserts.

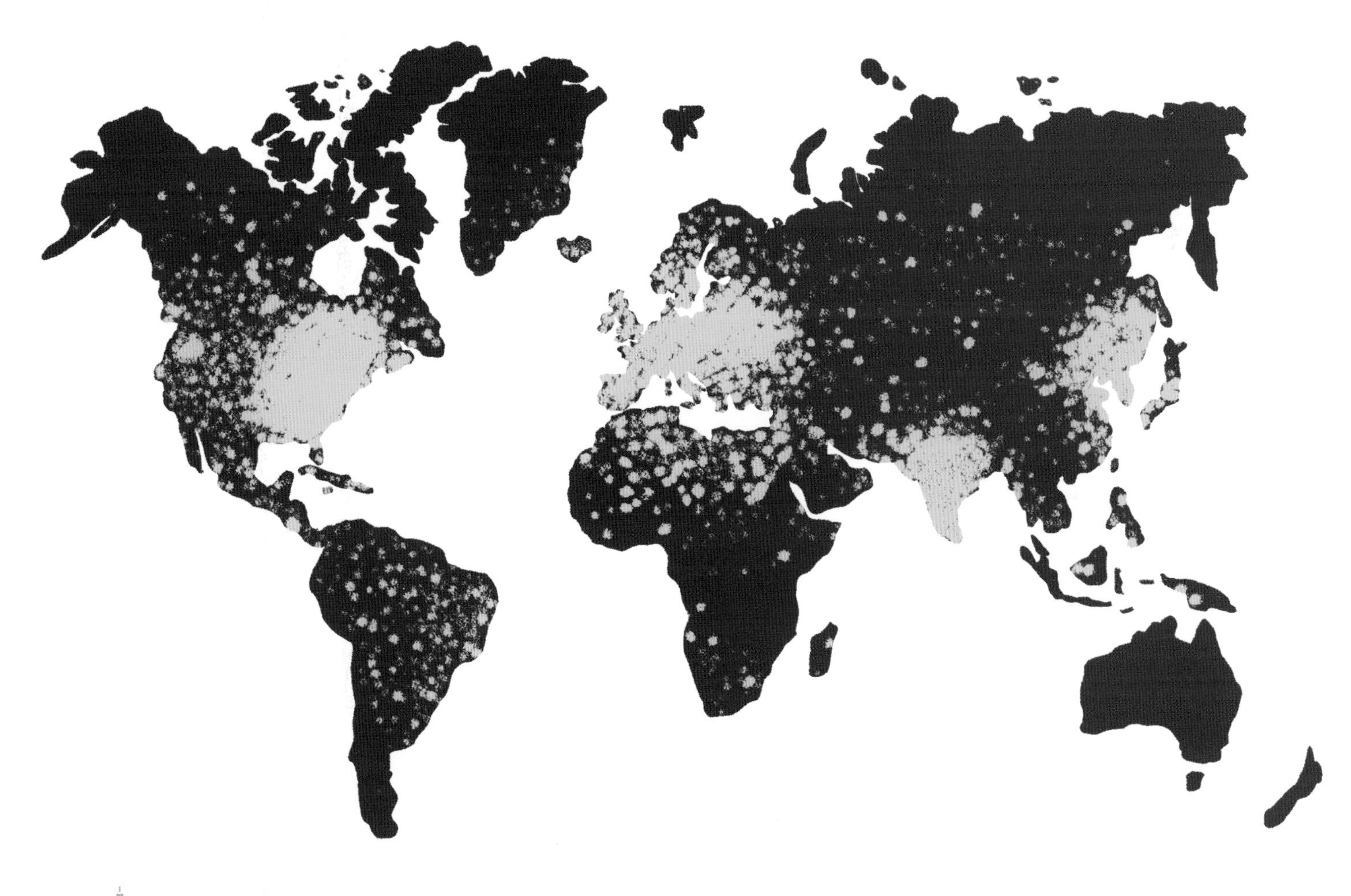

URBAN AREAS

Today, there are towns and cities all over the planet. More than 55 percent of the world's population live in cities, and it's increasing every year.

Satellites can show us the world's towns, cities, and built-up areas by detecting electric lights at night. This map shows the patterns of lights.

THE MODERN WORLD

In just the last few hundred years, the planet has been changed more than ever, thanks to modern inventions like engines, electrical power, aircraft, and computers.

THE INDUSTRIAL REVOLUTION

The Industrial Revolution is a name for a big change in the way we make and do things. It began in Europe in the 1700s, and gradually spread around the world. Just like changes in prehistoric times, it was driven by our brilliant brains coming up with new ideas and inventions—but the results are not all good.

WHAT CHANGED?

Before the Industrial Revolution, most things were made on a small scale. Craftspeople sewed clothes and made pottery, farmers farmed small areas of land, and books were hand-printed one at a time. Travel was by boat or horse-drawn cart. Lights were candles and oil lamps, and household tasks took ages as they had to be done by hand.

In the 1700s and 1800s, advances in science and new discoveries paved the way for new inventions that created the modern world that we live in today. For example …

NEW MATERIALS AND BUILDING METHODS MEANT THAT WE COULD BUILD TALLER AND TALLER SKYSCRAPERS.

WE BURNED MORE AND MORE FUEL, WHICH BEGAN TO POLLUTE THE AIR.

WE BEGAN USING MACHINES TO MAKE THINGS IN FACTORIES, INSTEAD OF MAKING THEM BY HAND.

WE INVENTED ENGINES THAT COULD BURN FUEL SUCH AS COAL AND GAS TO MAKE MACHINES WORK.

MACHINERY AND VEHICLES MADE IT EASIER TO GROW AND TRANSPORT FOOD.

MORE AND MORE!

Thanks to all these changes, we've ended up taking over even MORE wild land for our houses, factories, shopping malls, roads, and airports, and creating more pollution and waste as we make more and more stuff.

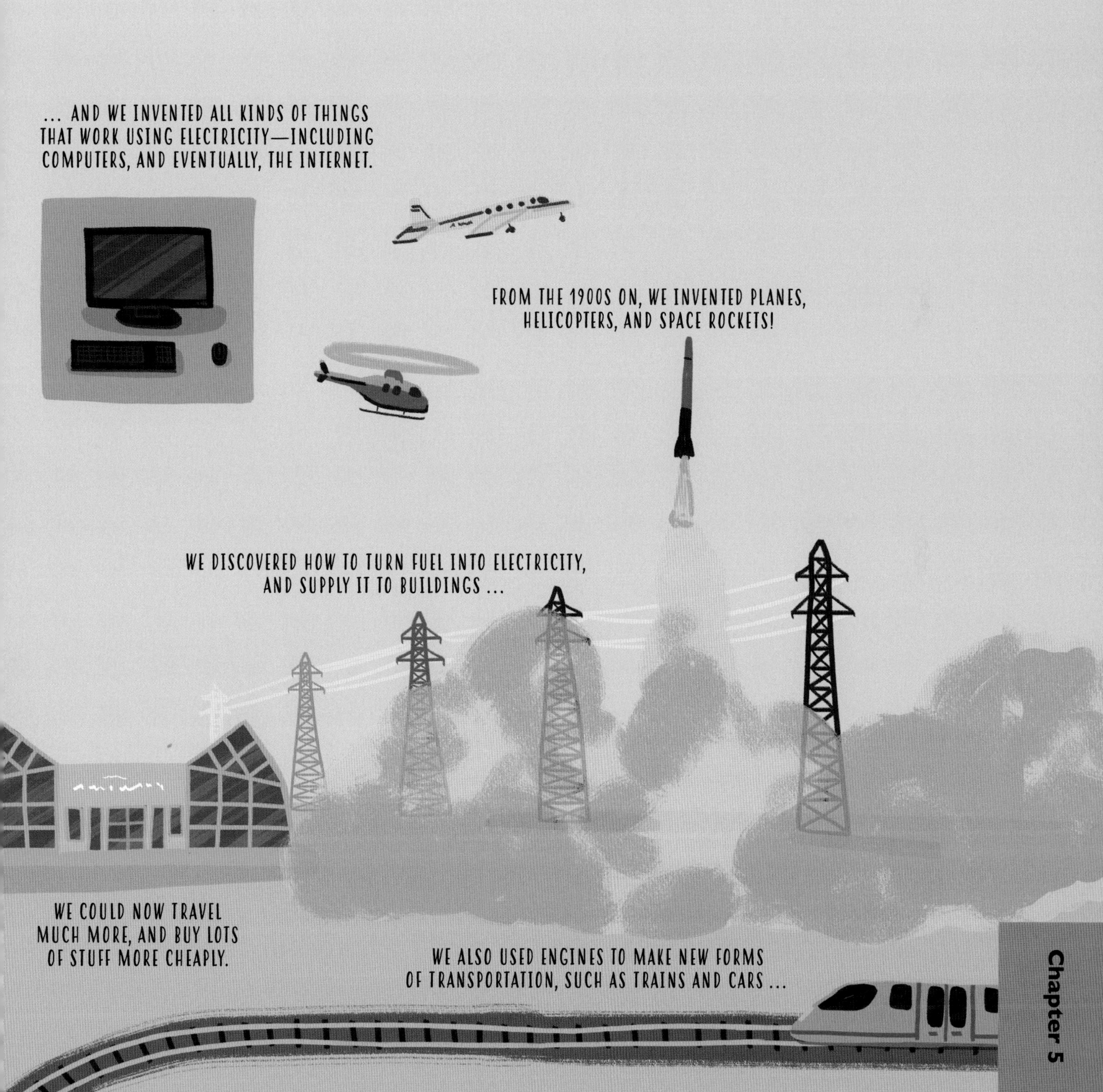

CHANGING NATURE

Have you ever wondered why you don't see black-and-white cows, broccoli, or poodles in the wild? It's because they don't exist in the wild! Humans created them by domesticating, or changing, wild living things.

SELECTIVE BREEDING

We didn't make these changes all at once. They happened slowly, through a process called **selective breeding**. It's basically a kind of evolution that humans control.

To do it, you start with a wild plant or animal, such as einkorn, that provides something useful—in this case, its seeds, which are good for eating.

WILD EINKORN HAS A SMALL SEED HEAD WITH SMALL SEEDS.

PICK THE BEST!

Thanks to slight changes in DNA (see page 72), some einkorn plants naturally have bigger seeds than others. So you choose plants with the biggest, plumpest seeds, and plant them. They should pass on their DNA and grow into more einkorn with large seeds.

Next time, you pick the biggest seeds from that crop—and so on, and so on. Over many generations, you make the plant evolve in a useful way, to provide as much food as possible.

MODERN WHEAT, WHICH WE USE TO MAKE BREAD, FLOUR, AND PASTA, WAS MADE BY SELECTIVE BREEDING OF WILD EINKORN.

WILD MOUFLON

WONDERFUL WOOL

Most farm animals and crops are domesticated versions of wild creatures. Farm sheep, for example, were bred from a type of wild sheep called a mouflon. Sheep can be farmed for meat, but also for their wool—so they were bred to have thick, soft coats.

DOMESTIC SHEEP

WILD WOLF

OUR BEST FRIENDS

We've also domesticated some animals, such as dogs, to be our helpers and pets. All the different breeds of dogs were bred from a wild wolf species. Wolves probably began hanging around human homes looking for food, or following human hunters, thousands of years ago. Since then, selective breeding for different qualities has created many different kinds of dogs, such as guard dogs, sniffer dogs, guide dogs, and cuddly pet dogs.

DOMESTIC DOG

OUT OF CURIOSITY

We've also created new materials, by changing and processing natural ones. Plastic was first invented in the 1850s, and is made from mineral oil, a natural resource. It's very useful, but doesn't rot easily—so waste plastic has caused a huge plastic litter problem around the world.

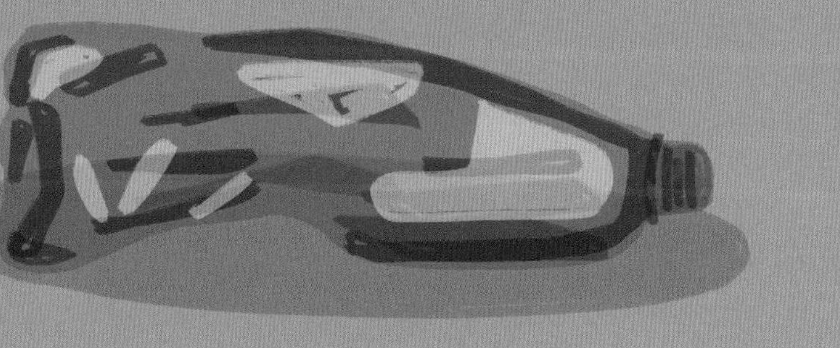

MAKING MAPS

Maps are an important part of studying and understanding the Earth. Humans have been making maps for thousands of years. The earliest known map, showing part of a valley in what is now France, is carved on a stone slab, and dates from around 1800 BCE.

WHAT ARE MAPS FOR?

A map is like a diagram of a part of the Earth. It can show all kinds of different information, such as the height of the land, the natural surroundings such as forests, rocks, and water, footpaths, buildings, and roads, weather patterns, or even underground rocks.

Earth scientists use maps a lot to study and show different things about the Earth. But they're also useful for everyone else, for finding our way, and checking where things are.

OLD AND NEW

Although some ancient maps were carved in stone, for most of history they've been drawn and printed on paper. Today, we also have digital maps on computers and phones.

REAL WORLD, MAP WORLD

Here, you can see a picture of a real landscape and, on the opposite page, a map showing the same area from above.

MAP SCALES

We draw maps using a scale, meaning that the same distance on the map always stands for the same distance in real life. For example, one square on this map stands for a 50 x 50 m (164 x 164 ft) square in the real landscape.

MAP LEGENDS

A map's legend or key shows you what the symbols or patterns on the map stand for. For example, in our map, they are:

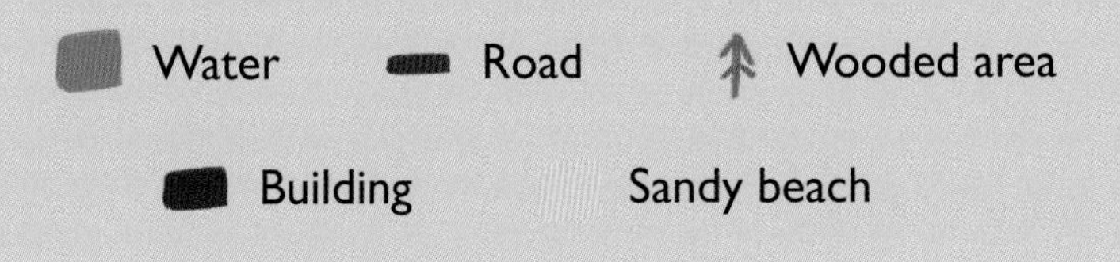

CONTOUR LINES

Contour lines are a way of showing slopes and hills on a flat map. Each line connects points of the same **altitude**, or height above sea level. A set of rings getting smaller and smaller toward the middle could show a hill or mountain.

COORDINATES

Coordinates help you find a point on a map. The map is covered in a grid of lines, which are given numbers or letters. So, for example, in this map, the house that is closest to the river is in square C4.

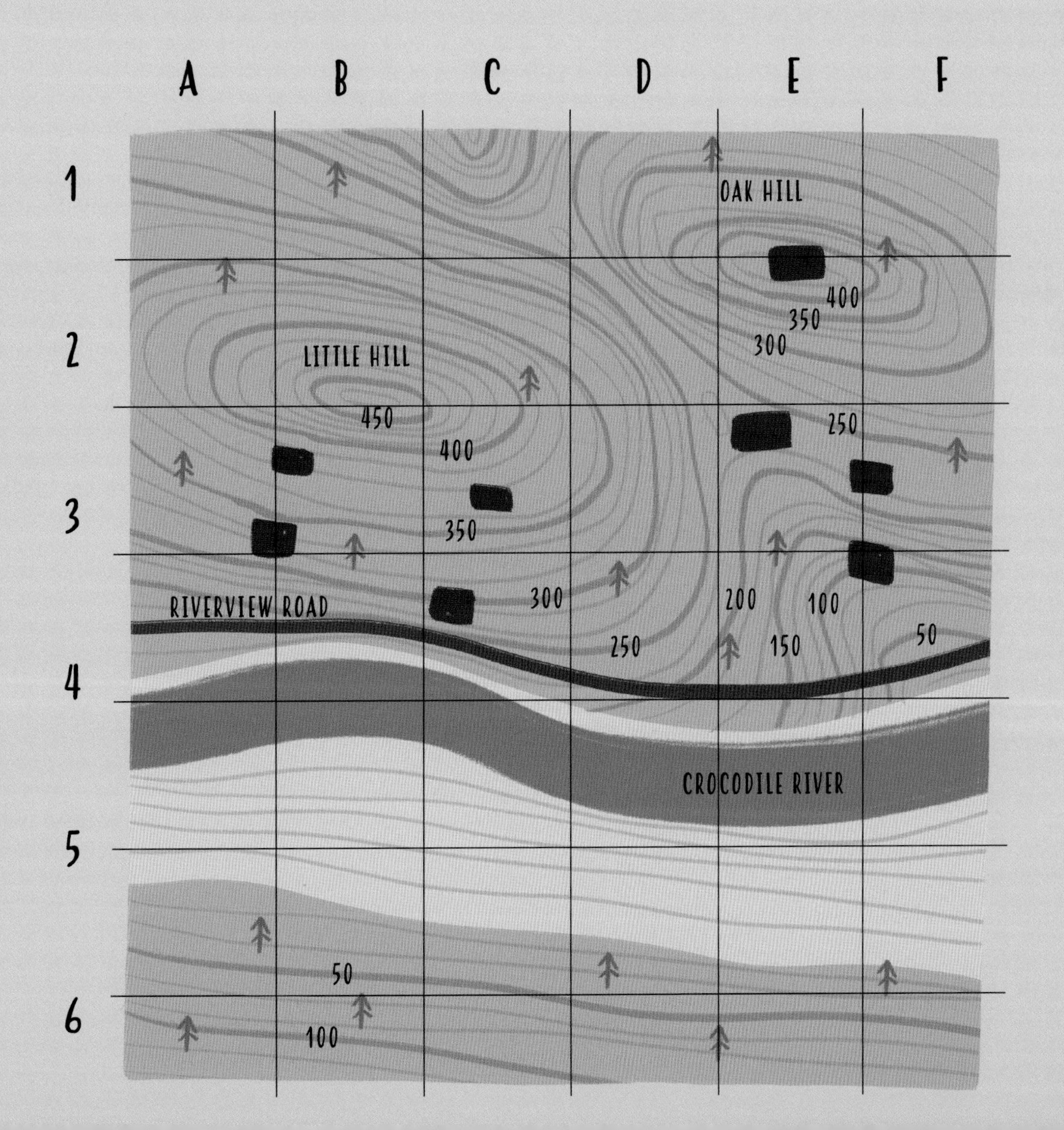

CHAPTER 6

SAVING THE EARTH

Humans have made so many changes to the world that we've caused a lot of problems. Destroying vast areas of natural wildlife habitat has driven some wild species to extinction, while others are endangered and at risk of dying out. We've used up huge amounts of natural resources like fish, trees, and rare minerals. We've polluted the planet with chemicals from farms and factories, litter, plastic waste, and sewage. And, we've burned so much fuel that the waste gases released into the air are making the planet heat up, causing climate change.

What can we do? In this chapter, we'll explore how the planet has been harmed, and how we're trying to fix it.

CROWDED PLANET

One of the biggest problems for our planet is the enormous number of people now living on Earth. Since the Industrial Revolution, the human population has shot up. Of course, there are large numbers of other living things, too—but they don't take up as much space as we do, nor do they cause pollution like we do.

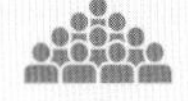

POPULATION BOOM

In 10,000 BCE, around the time that farming began, experts think there were somewhere between one million and 10 million people on the planet. That sounds like a lot, but they were spread out all over the world. Today, there can be over 10 million people in a single big city, such as Tokyo or New York.

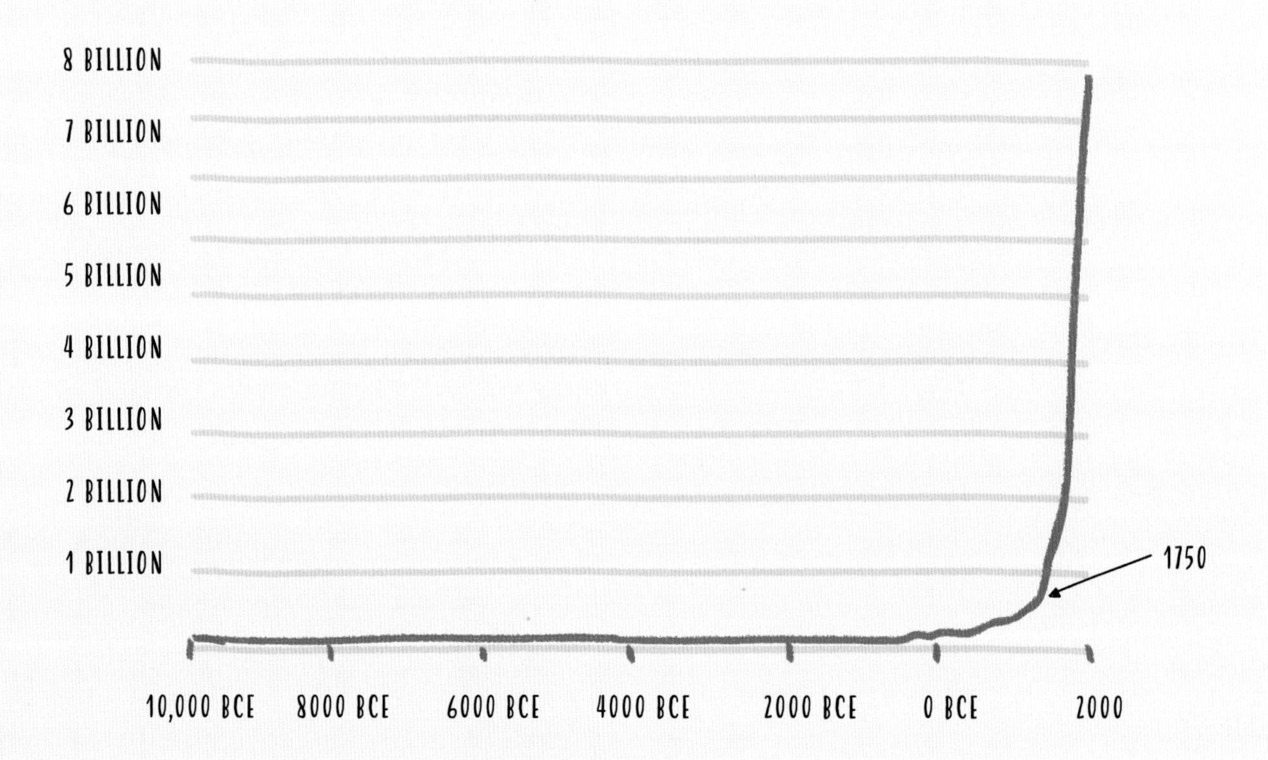

In 1750, just before the start of the Industrial Revolution, there were around 600–900 million people on Earth. That's a lot more, but still under one billion (1,000,000,000).

Today, less than 300 years later, there are 7.9 billion—and it's still going up.

HOW DID IT HAPPEN?

Basically, over time, humans have become better and better at surviving. And this has been especially true since the Industrial Revolution brought changes like cheaper food, warmer, safer homes, running water, and flushing toilets. We've also invented medicines such as antibiotics and vaccinations, saving us from many deadly diseases. Not everyone in the world has all these things, but they have made a big difference. More and more people have survived long enough to grow up and have their own children, and the population has exploded.

TAKING UP SPACE

Of course, that's good news in one way. We can treat illnesses, get enough food, and have happier, easier lives. But since there are so many people who need homes, food, and goods, it means we're using up more resources and space than ever.

In some big cities, a lot of people live in densely packed, high-rise apartment buildings like these, since it's the only way to fit everyone in.

ENERGY AND ELECTRICITY

Energy means things such as light, heat, sound, and movement. Moving around in a car, cooking something in a hot oven, or switching on an electric light, shower, or heater all use energy. Electricity is a type of energy, and we use it to power many kinds of machines and gadgets.

FROM THEN ...

In prehistoric times, humans didn't use as much energy as we do today. They burned wood for heat and light, but they didn't travel far, and didn't have electricity.

... TO NOW

Today, not only are there a lot more people on Earth, but each of us uses lots more energy. We use it to heat our homes, travel around in cars, trains, and planes, and to power household machines, electric lights, phones, and computer systems.

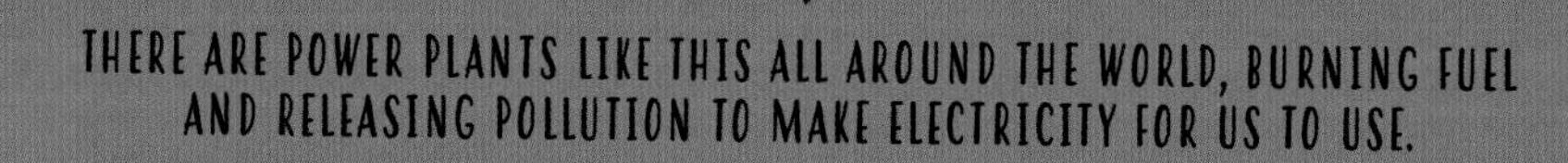

THERE ARE POWER PLANTS LIKE THIS ALL AROUND THE WORLD, BURNING FUEL AND RELEASING POLLUTION TO MAKE ELECTRICITY FOR US TO USE.

MANY PEOPLE HAVE AN ELECTRIC MIXER LIKE THIS AT HOME, FOR MIXING BAKING INGREDIENTS TOGETHER. IT MAKES THE JOB EASIER, BUT IT'S NOT ESSENTIAL. LONG AGO, PEOPLE JUST USED A WOODEN SPOON AND LOTS OF EFFORT!

GETTING ENOUGH ENERGY

All this energy has to come from somewhere. You can't make energy from nothing—you can only turn one kind of energy into another. For example, a car engine burns fuel to make the wheels turn. We can also burn fuel to power a generator, which creates a flow of electricity supply to houses.

The fuels we burn are mainly fossil fuels extracted from underground, such as coal, oil, or natural gas. Burning fuels like this creates pollution and adds to global warming.

A SCOOTER LIKE THIS RUNS ON ELECTRICITY, AND YOU CHARGE IT UP FROM AN ELECTRIC SOCKET. THE SCOOTER ITSELF DOESN'T RELEASE POLLUTION, BUT IF THE ELECTRICITY COMES FROM A FUEL-POWERED POWER PLANT, IT STILL ADDS TO THE POLLUTION IN THE AIR.

ELECTRICAL APPLIANCES SUCH AS WASHING MACHINES ARE VERY USEFUL BECAUSE THEY DO JOBS THAT USED TO TAKE PEOPLE HOURS AND HOURS OF WORK.

POLLUTION

Pollution is any harmful substance that's released into the environment, or surroundings. There are many different types of pollution, and most of them come from us humans and our modern inventions and activities.

BURNING FUEL

One of the biggest causes of pollution is burning fuel. As things like wood, gas, or coal burn, a chemical reaction happens. It gives out heat energy, which makes things like car engines or power plants work. But it also releases waste chemicals into the air. They add to global warming, but can cause other problems, too.

Exhaust gases from fuel-burning vehicles pollute the air in cities and around busy roads. The pollution includes poisonous gases and tiny, harmful soot particles. They can cause asthma and other lung diseases in humans and animals. They harm plants, too, by clogging their leaves and making it harder for them to soak up sunlight.

OUT OF CURIOSITY

Even our sounds and lights can cause pollution! Noisy ship engines interfere with the sounds whales and dolphins make to call to each other. And our bright electric lights confuse night insects like moths and fireflies, making it harder for them to find mates and breed.

WATER POLLUTION

We also release lots of pollution into rivers and seas. It comes from factory waste, littering, and farm chemicals, such as fertilizers and pesticides, washing into rivers. It can also come from sewage, the waste from our toilets and sinks. This doesn't just contain human poop, which can carry harmful germs, but also cleaning chemicals, shower gel, and things that some people flush down toilets, like cotton swabs or buds and disposable wipes.

We have sewage treatment plants that are supposed to clean the water before it can escape into the environment. But in many places, this doesn't happen, and the sewage just flows straight into rivers or the sea.

Water pollution can kill water wildlife, as well as making the water dangerous for people to drink or swim in.

LITTER

Litter is ugly and messy, but it can cause other problems, too. Animals sometimes swallow it by accident, blocking their stomachs so that they can't eat. Wires or old fishing nets can get tangled around animals, killing or injuring them. Someone dropping a hot cigarette can start a wildfire. So can curved glass bottles, which can magnify the Sun's heat and set dry plants alight.

Sea turtles sometimes swallow plastic bags, maybe because they resemble tasty-looking jellyfish.

THE GREENHOUSE EFFECT

One type of air pollution is causing a very big problem by making the Earth heat up. This is called global warming, and it happens because of the greenhouse effect.

HOW IT WORKS

Burning fuel releases waste gases, including a lot of one particular gas, carbon dioxide. Carbon dioxide is known as a greenhouse gas. Like the glass in a greenhouse, it lets light in but keeps heat from getting out.

1 INFRARED LIGHT FROM THE SUN HITS THE EARTH.

2 IT GETS ABSORBED INTO THE GROUND, AND HEATS IT UP.

3 HEAT FROM THE GROUND WARMS THE AIR.

4 CARBON DIOXIDE IN THE ATMOSPHERE SOAKS UP THIS HEAT ENERGY, THEN RELEASES IT, MAKING THE ATMOSPHERE STAY WARM.

KEEPING COZY

The **greenhouse effect** is not a bad thing in itself. The atmosphere naturally contains some carbon dioxide, as well as smaller amounts of other greenhouse gases. Water vapor also acts as a greenhouse gas. The greenhouse effect has always helped keep the world warm enough for life to survive.

COW BURPS

Carbon dioxide is one important greenhouse gas. But there's another one that is adding to global warming, called methane. It's released from trash rotting in landfill sites, and when we extract and process fossil fuels. It also comes from some types of farming.

Farm animals such as cows release a lot of methane as they burp and fart while chewing and digesting grass.

5

SOME HEAT ESCAPES BACK INTO SPACE.

TOO MUCH GAS!

The problem is that the atmosphere now contains extra greenhouse gases from pollution. As the amount of carbon dioxide increases, so does the Earth's average temperature. Since the Industrial Revolution began, it has increased by about 1°C (1.8°F), and it's still going up. That sounds like a small amount, but it's having a big effect on the planet's icy areas, weather, seas and oceans, and climate.

CLIMATE CHANGE

Global warming doesn't just make the world hotter. It's also changing climates around the world in a variety of different ways—and many of them can be damaging or dangerous.

WILDFIRES IN AUSTRALIA ARE BECOMING BIGGER AND MORE FREQUENT AS THE AVERAGE TEMPERATURE INCREASES.

HEAT AND DROUGHT

Some parts of the world, such as Australia and the western United States, are getting warmer and drier weather, including more heatwaves in summer. This can lead to many different problems, including:

- People suffering from dehydration and heatstroke
- Water shortages for people and animals
- Droughts that kill crops
- More wildfires, which threaten lives, damage homes, and destroy animal habitats.

ICE AND WATER

The extra heat also has a big effect on the world's ice sheets, ice caps, and glaciers. They're starting to melt, and some smaller areas of ice are disappearing. The melted ice flows into rivers and ends up in the sea. Gradually, this adds more water to the sea, making sea levels higher. At the same time, as the oceans warm, the water expands, taking up more space—and rises higher still.

As the sea level rises, big waves and sea storms cause more damage and flooding on the land. Eventually, low-lying islands and coastal areas could start to disappear underwater as the sea covers them.

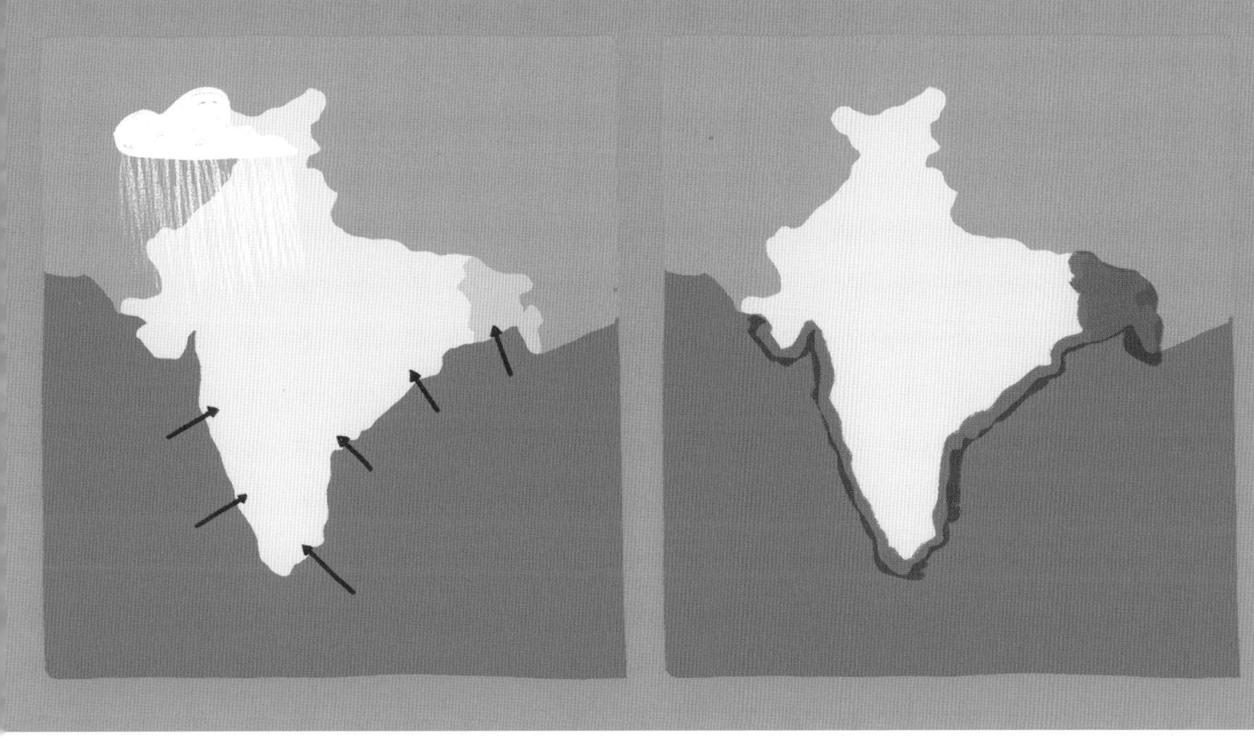

This map shows how the coastline of India and Bangladesh could change if the sea level rose by 20 m (65 ft).

STORMS AND FLOODS

In some other places, global warming is causing more powerful windstorms, heavy rain, and flooding, This is because when it's warmer, more water evaporates from the sea, creating more rain clouds, and bigger cyclones and hurricanes.

Cyclones, typhoons, and hurricanes can form over the ocean when the water is warmer than about 27°C (81°F). Global warming is increasing ocean temperatures, making these storms more likely and more powerful.

ENDANGERED SPECIES

An endangered species is a species (or type) of living thing that is in danger of dying out and becoming extinct. Once that happens, that species can never come back.

COMING AND GOING

Throughout the history of life on Earth, new species have evolved and old ones have gone extinct. That's natural and normal. Each species typically survives for a few million years before dying out. That's why we're not still surrounded by dinosaurs!

EXTINCTION EPIDEMIC

However, since humans began taking over the planet, species have been dying out much faster than normal, since we've made it harder for them to survive. Many species are now endangered, and at risk of dying out.

THREATS TO WILDLIFE

How are we causing this? The main reasons are:

- Habitat loss—when we destroy wild habitats to make space for human homes and farms
- Pollution damaging living things and their habitats
- Climate change damaging habitats or making it hard to live there
- Hunting—killing animals to eat, for body parts like skins and tusks, or even for fun
- Collecting—taking animals from the wild to keep in collections or to sell as pets

OUT OF CURIOSITY

To keep track of the problem, scientists monitor and count wild animals, then give each species a status that show how endangered it is, such as:

LC..... Least Concern (not endangered)

NT..... Near Threatened (could become endangered soon)

VU..... Vulnerable (at some risk)

EN..... Endangered

CR .... Critically (extremely) Endangered

GOING, GOING, GONE?

Meet a selection of endangered species from around the world—before it's too late!

CONSERVATION

Conservation means preserving or saving something. It's what we need to do to help the Earth, its habitats, and wildlife recover from some of the problems we've caused. There are now lots of conservation campaigns and schemes around the world, but we still need to do more.

CONSERVATION METHODS

There are many different ways of doing conservation. International organizations, governments, and wildlife charities often work together to try and make them happen. They include ...

Setting up wildlife reserves—areas of natural wild land or sea that are set aside for wildlife, with no building, hunting, farming, or mining allowed.

Making laws against hunting, collecting, or harming wild animals, especially endangered species.

Making laws against littering and pollution, and cleaning up pollution that's already there.

Replanting forests, and other natural habitats such as seagrass meadows in shallow seas.

Breeding endangered species in captivity, then releasing them into the wild to help increase their populations.

Finding ways to use less space for farming, such as agroforestry (combining farming with wild forests).

ECOTOURISM

Ecotourism is a way of helping to look after endangered species and habitats. Tourists pay to visit wildlife preserves (or reserves) and see the plants and animals there. This gives local people jobs, raises money to run the reserves, and teaches visitors about conservation. However, we have to do it carefully, since too many visitors could cause more damage and pollution.

OUT OF CURIOSITY

Here are some of the ways everyone can help with wildlife conservation:

- **Don't drop litter.**
- **Avoid disposable plastic items like water bottles—use a reuseable one instead.**
- **Don't pick wild flowers or bother wild animals.**
- **If you have outdoor space, leave part of it to grow wild to provide wildlife habitats.**
- **Plant a tree, if you can!**
- **Try to eat less meat—farming meat takes up more space than farming plants.**
- **Help on volunteerg days to pick up litter from beaches or parks.**
- **Visit wildlife preserves to go wildlife-spotting.**
- **Ask if your family or school class can adopt an animal in a preserve.**

TRADE BANS

People sometimes hunt endangered species, even when it's against the law, because they have valuable body parts, such as elephant tusks. They're used to make ivory objects such as knife handles and carvings. Countries around the world work together to make it illegal to trade, buy, or sell anything made from endangered species.

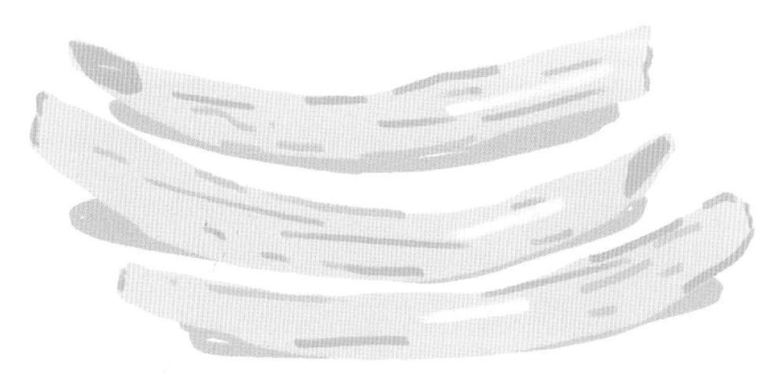

IVORY IS MADE FROM ELEPHANT TUSKS.

RENEWABLE ENERGY

One of the most important things we have to do is to burn less fuel. Burning fuel, especially fossil fuels such as coal, oil, and gas, is a big cause of pollution, and the main cause of global warming. So, we need to find new ways to make the electricity we need, and new ways to power our cars, buses, and other forms of transportation.

RENEWABLE ENERGY

Around the world, we're starting to switch to renewable energy sources. These use natural energy, such as wind, sunshine, and the flow of rivers, to make a supply of electricity. It's called "renewable" energy since there's always more of it, thanks to the Sun, the weather, and the water cycle.

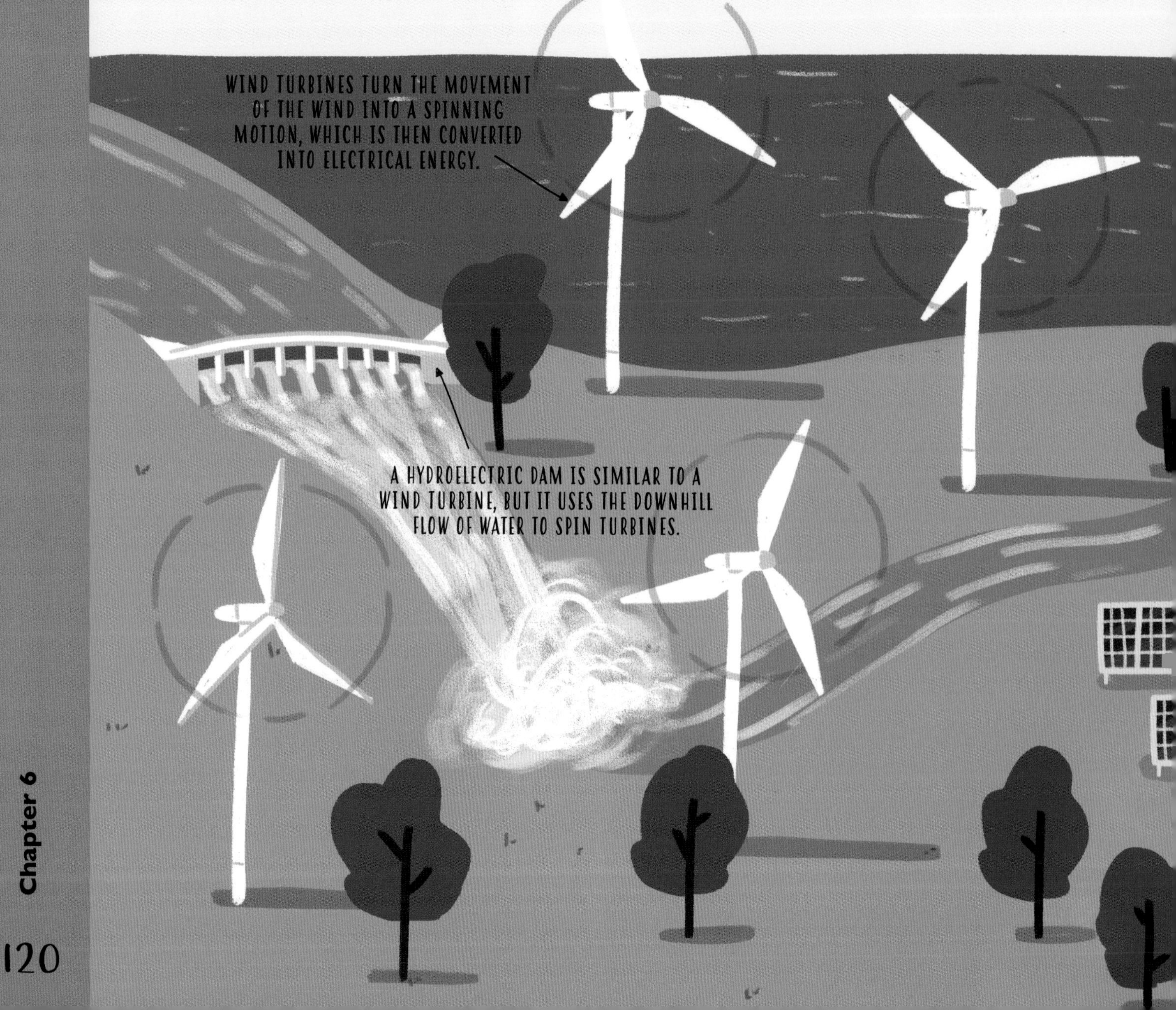

ELECTRIC TRANSPORTATION

Instead of using fuel-burning engines, we're now making electric cars, buses, and trains that can be charged up from an electricity supply. If the electricity they use comes from renewable sources, they create very little pollution.

We can also reduce pollution by walking and cycling around instead of using cars. It's healthier for our bodies, too.

ELECTRIC HOMES

At the moment, many people use fuels like gas, oil, wood, or coal for heating and cooking. We need to switch to renewable electricity for these things as well, so that we're not releasing pollution from our homes.

INTO THE FUTURE

What does the future hold for our beautiful, unique, life-filled planet?

No one knows for sure. Global warming and climate change will continue for awhile, since we can't stop them overnight. Gradually, we should be able to slow them down and limit the damage. Human population growth is also slowing down, and eventually it will start to shrink again. By planting more trees, restoring wild habitats, and cleaning up pollution, we can help the Earth return to a more natural, clean, green, and healthy state. And maybe we can use our big brains and inventing skills to come up with new ways to make clean energy, help wildlife, and fight climate change.

One day, we might even be able to travel to other planets and moons, and set up new homes there.

What might those worlds be like?

WORLD RECORDS

Here's an overview of Planet Earth's record-breaking mountains, rivers, lakes, deserts, and other incredible extremes.

BIGGEST LAKE

Caspian Sea, eastern Asia

Area: 386,400 km^2 (149,000 mi^2)

BIGGEST OCEAN

Pacific Ocean

Area: about 163,000,000 km^2 (63,000,000 mi^2)

BIGGEST ISLAND (NOT INCLUDING THE CONTINENTS)

Greenland, North America

Area of main island: 2,130,800 km^2 (822,700 mi^2)

DEEPEST LAKE

Lake Baikal, Russia

Maximum depth: 1,642 m (5,387 ft)

DEEPEST POINT IN THE OCEAN

Challenger Deep, in the Mariana Trench, Pacific Ocean

Depth: 10,994 m (36,070 ft)

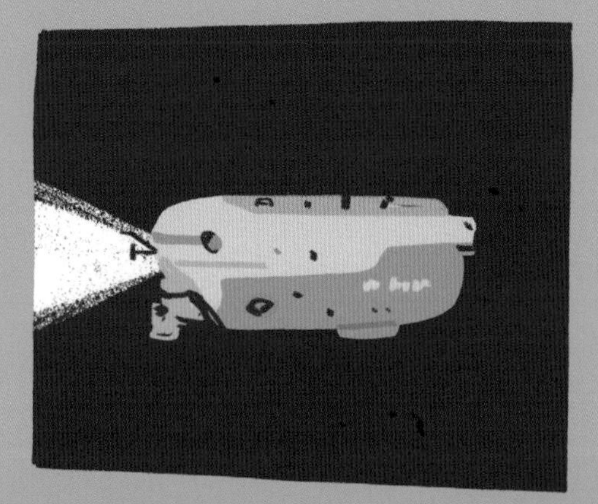

HIGHEST MOUNTAIN ABOVE SEA LEVEL

Mount Everest, on the border of Nepal and China

Height: 8,848 m (29,031 ft)

HIGHEST MOUNTAIN FROM BASE TO PEAK

Mauna Kea, Hawaii

Height from seabed: 9,966 m (32,696 ft)

HIGHEST VOLCANO ABOVE SEA LEVEL

Ojos del Salado, on the border of Argentina and Chile

Height: 6,893 m (22,615 ft)

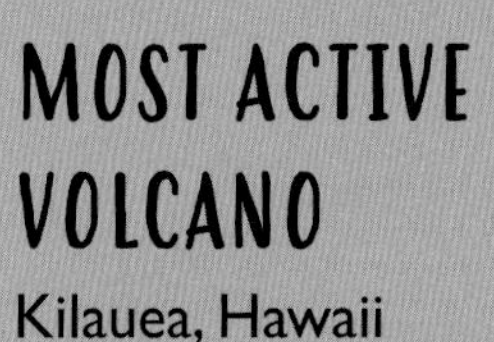

MOST ACTIVE VOLCANO

Kilauea, Hawaii

DRIEST DESERT

Atacama Desert, Chile

Average annual rainfall: About 15 mm (0.6 in)

BIGGEST DESERT*

Sahara Desert, northern Africa

Area: about 9.1 million km^2 (3.5 million mi^2)

*Some scientists say Antarctica is the biggest desert, since it's so cold that the water there is mostly ice. However, the Sahara is the biggest non-polar desert.

COLDEST RECORDED TEMPERATURE ON THE EARTH'S SURFACE

–89.2 °C (–128.6 °F) at Vostok research station, Antarctica, July 21, 1983

HOTTEST RECORDED TEMPERATURE ON THE EARTH'S SURFACE

(56.7 °C) (134 °F) at Death Valley, California, USA, July 10, 1913

LONGEST RIVER

River Nile, Africa

Length: about 6, 650 km (4,130 mi)

BIGGEST POPULATION

China, Asia

Population: about 1.42 billion

HIGHEST WATERFALL

Angel Falls, Venezuela

Height: 979 m (3,212 ft)

BIGGEST COUNTRY

Russia, Europe and Asia

Area: about 17,125,000 km^2 (6,612, 000 mi^2)

GLOSSARY

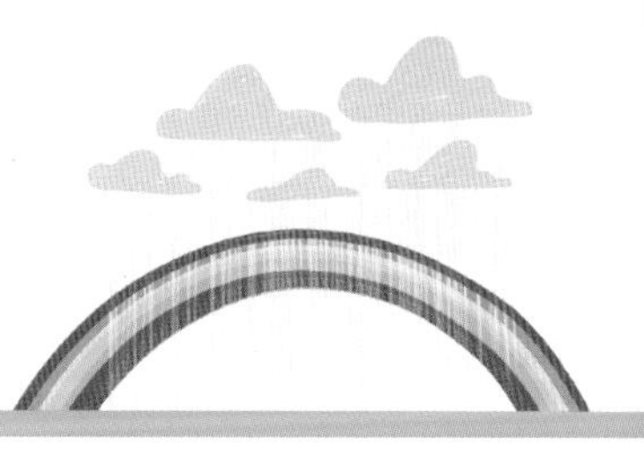

altitude: Height above sea level.

aquifer: An area of underground soil or rock that contains groundwater.

archaea: A group of microscopic, single-celled living things similar to bacteria.

bacteria: A group of microscopic, single-celled living things with no cell nucleus. Some can cause diseases, but others can be helpful to other living things.

biodiversity: The variety of life, either on the whole planet or in a particular place.

biome: A large area with a particular type of climate, landscape, plants, and other wildlife.

chlorophyll: A green chemical found in plants, which they use in photosynthesis to help make their food.

condense: To change from a gas into a liquid.

continental island: An island that lies on the continental shelf, close to a continent.

continental shelf: A shallower part of the seabed found around continents and coasts.

contour lines: Lines on a map that connect points at the same altitude. These can be used to show slopes, mountains, and valleys.

convergent boundary: A place where two tectonic plates meet and push towards each other.

crevasse: A deep crack or gap in a glacier or ice sheet.

crust: The layer of solid rock surrounding the Earth.

cyclone: A large spinning windstorm that forms over warm ocean.

delta: A triangle-shaped area where a river flows into the sea, and mud and silt collect to form islands.

divergent boundary: A place where two tectonic plates are moving away from each other.

DNA (short for Deoxyribonucleic Acid): A string-shaped chemical that contains the instructions for how living things work and grow.

ecosystem: A habitat and the community of living things that live in it.

erosion: A process that happens when rock, sand, or other natural material gets carried from one place to another, for example by wind, water, or gravity.

estuary: A wide part of a river where it joins the sea.

extremophiles: Bacteria and archaea that thrive at extremely high or low temperatures, or other extreme conditions.

fossil: An impression, trace, or remains left in rock by a living thing.

fungi: A group of living things that includes mushrooms, molds, and yeast.

global warming: An increase in Earth's average temperature over the last two centuries, caused by human activity.

gravity: A natural force created around objects with mass, which draws other objects toward them. Earth's gravity is what keeps us on the ground, and what makes objects fall.

greenhouse effect: The way some gases in Earth's atmosphere trap heat, increasing global warming.

groundwater: Water held in underground rocks and soil.

habitat: The natural home or surroundings of a living thing.

humidity: The amount of water vapor (water in the form of a gas) held in the air.

hyphae: Hairlike roots used by some fungi to collect food.

infrared: An invisible kind of light energy that makes things warm up.

invertebrate: An animal without a backbone.

karst: A type of landscape containing mostly limestone rock, with a lot of caves, underground tunnels, and rivers.

magma: Very hot, molten, or partly molten rock inside the Earth.

mantle: The thick layer of rock inside the Earth, between the crust and the core.

meteorologist: A scientist who studies and predicts weather.

mineral: A natural, nonliving substance from the Earth that is the same all the way through.

nonporous rock: Rock that cannot soak up water.

nutrients: Chemicals or substances that act as food for living things.

oceanic island: An island in the open ocean, that rises from the deep seabed.

orbit: To circle around another object, for example, when a moon orbits a planet.

photosynthesis: The process of using energy from the Sun to turn water and carbon dioxide gas into food, which happens inside a plant's leaves.

plate boundary: A line where two tectonic plates meet.

porous rock: Rock that contains tiny gaps or pores (holes), meaning it can soak up water.

sediment: Sand, pebbles, mud, seashells, or other material that settles and collects in layers, especially on the seabed.

selective breeding: Choosing the most useful animals or plants to breed from, which can make a living species change over time.

sonar: A way of measuring the seabed or finding objects underwater, by sending out sounds and detecting the echoes that come back.

species: The scientific name for a particular type of living thing.

tectonic plates: The huge sections of rock that make up the Earth's crust.

tsunami: A fast-moving wave caused by a sudden movement of a large amount of seawater.

turbine: A device that uses a movement, such as the flow of wind or water, to make a wheel spin, which is then used to generate electricity.

ultraviolet light: An invisible type of light energy that can cause sunburn.

vertebrate: An animal with a backbone.

wavelength: The length of a wave, from the peak of one wave to the peak of the next.

weathering: The process of weather and other forces breaking down and wearing away rock.

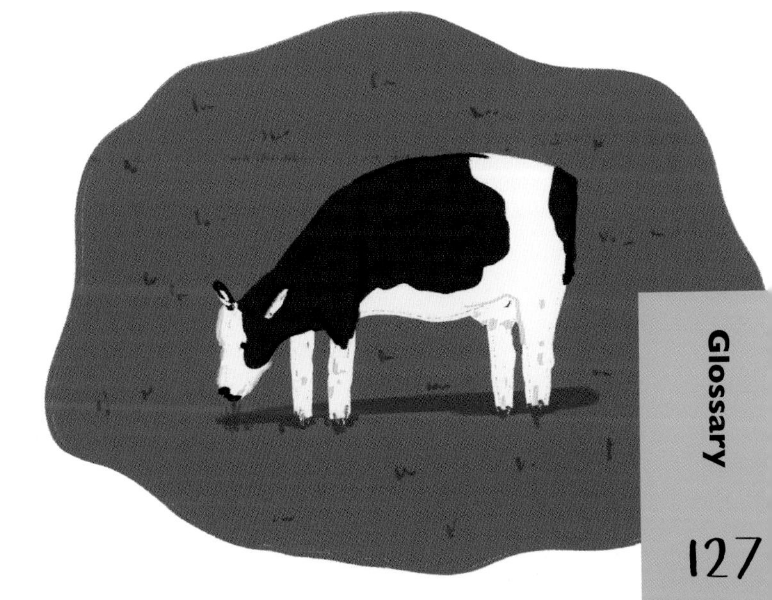

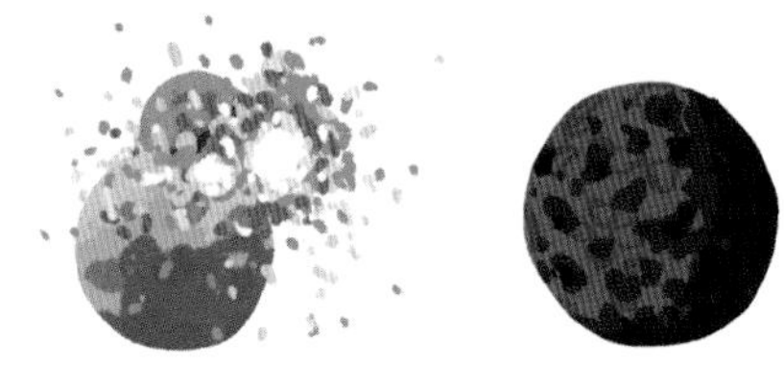

INDEX

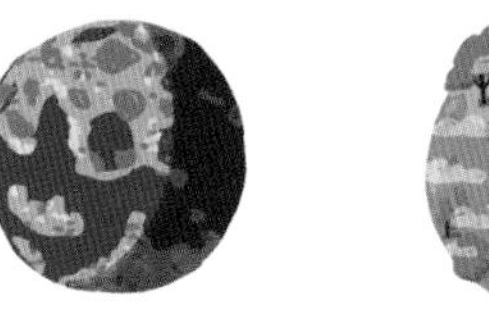